I0411157

How To Survive
# When The Dollar Dies
## A Financial Battle Plan
by

## Dr. Solomon Greenburg

© 2013 2ndEmpireMedia.Com

Printed in the United States of America

# Dedication

This book is dedicated to my wonderful, Godly, wife, who has diligently studied the financial consultants and gathered the information and without whom we would not have survived the 2008 mortgage and real estate crisis and this information would not have been available to me.

It is the diligent application of the principals and information, including the intrinsic knowledge necessary to understand banking history and the creation of fiat currency that have allowed us to survive the financial problems caused by government and banking arrogance.

We expect, by applying these principles, to ride out the greater wave of economic destruction to come.

In this book, you will learn how to recognize America's current and coming monetary problems and ways you can protect yourself from the inevitable financial meltdown; the disappearing dollar.

You will gain some understanding about the history of money, different forms of money, and the history of banking.

It is our intent to survive the demise of the dollar and all the financial repercussions that result from that demise.

God is in the details, *man is in the way*.

# Contents

# About the Author:

My father was a good Democrat. He was also a laborer. He felt one needed to work, but the government needed to provide financial security. He was never taught how to be successful and never had the mindset of abundance.

I grew up watching a man who meant well squander his talents, which were many, and his fairly good income as a machinist, on little personal rewards, whether it was buying novels and comic books, or gambling what little he had away at some of the casinos in Reno or Tahoe (he did not drink and no one could figure out what else he could have spent his money on). He always had a dream, but never quite seemed to understand that he had to fulfill that dream himself; with minimal outside assistance.

Since I never had the benefit of a mentor, or even the idea that I needed a mentor, to overcome the perpetuation of failing, I was forced to serve the apprenticeship of hard knocks.

Assisted by marrying an intelligent and industrious German woman, I managed to learn there was more to life than a nine-to-five job and paying the tax man. I moved out of the rat race in 1978 and became a real estate broker.

Being in a small Northern California community, I was pushed into learning all aspects of real estate, which included residential, commercial, private financing, spec building, and multi-family income properties.

After thirty-five years of being a broker and, like so many others, seeing the retirement investments we made go up in smoke with the 2008 fiasco in the subprime mortgage industry and the subsequent corporate welfare, we started to look for more savvy, learned people from whom to seek advice and direction.

We have managed to land on our feet, through all the rough financial terrain, and have set our sights on overcoming the ignorance that our social contract has forced upon us.

It is with all that in mind I have decided to help others who are looking for some kind of direction; some kind of salvation from the current dog-eat-dog environment. This book is that attempt. This book is not necessarily for the wealthy, for the principles apply to all.

It is my goal to help the blue collar worker; the middle class family that has amassed a small retirement account and perhaps has managed to pick up a few stocks or a little real estate along the way. This is the advice I would give to myself.

Surprise yourself and the world by surviving the coming destruction of the dollar along with virtually every major currency in the world.

# Is Western Civilization
# The Cause Or The Cure?

**Hyper Inflation in the Last 100 Years**
Hyperinflation is just another name for "runaway inflation" (*on steroids*). The Cambridge Online Dictionary defines Hyperinflation as
*"a condition where the price of everything in a national economy goes out of control and increases very quickly."*

The episodes of hyperinflation, in history, were primarily because of a rapidly accelerating, increase in the supply of money (rampant printing) that wasn't matched by a corresponding increase in goods and services in countries where hyperinflation has occurred, the cost of food and goods increased so much that the money of those countries rapidly became worthless.

In fact, there have been cases where the money of a country experiencing hyperinflation was used for starting fires and heating homes in wood and coal-fired residential heaters/stoves, because the value of the money was less than the value of commodities like wood and coal.

A surprising statistic from the Cato Journal shows there have been as many as 56 countries that have gone through devastating hyperinflation periods in the last 100 years. Some you may have heard about, but many you probably have not.

The American government seems to think it is immune to the ravages of decimating its own currency. Pretty much everyone grasps the idea that, the more there is of an item, the less valuable each item becomes. That is the concept behind buying a large quantity of something. The more we buy of anything, the less each of the items we are purchasing costs.

The more demand there is for something, the more valuable or costly it becomes. That is until the supply, which had to be increased to meet the demand, outstrips the demand.

The dollars has had the privilege of being the reserve currency for many years. That means the dollar has been in high demand, because everything that is purchased in the world is settled up in dollars.

If Germany purchases a barrel of oil from Saudi Arabia, that oil has to be purchased in dollars. In order to do that, Germany has to exchange their euros into dollars (which has a transaction or exchange fee charged by the US government), which are then used to pay to the Saudis and who are then compelled to exchange the US dollars into their currency (which incurs another transaction or exchange fee).

That process has allowed the USA to print more money, out of thin air, with impunity, because it is the dollar that the world recognizes as the basic medium of exchange.

Although printing more of the paper money (and oddly enough today's printing of money does not always require paper, but only requires the Federal Reserve to digitally issue a credit to whomever they wish, usually banks, bonds brokers, and large corporations) weakens the value of each dollar, which in turn weakens the purchasing power of that dollar, it is exactly that madness that our government embraces as the instrument of hope.

Today the dollar is experiencing a strengthening, but it is not because the value of the dollar is growing, it is because the value of other currencies, against which the dollar is measured, is declining faster than the dollar.

The current administration of this country (2015) wrongly assumes it is their erroneous policies that are increasing the value of the dollar, but that is merely wishful thinking.

Have you noticed the increase in the price of food (often the number one cause of and lead-in to hyperinflation), whether in a grocery store or in a restaurant?

A restaurant meal that, as recently as a year or two ago, cost us $8.00 in a typical family restaurant now costs us between $10.00 and $12.00. That is a 50%+ increase in just a year or two. That is a pretty good start on our own road to inflation.

## Germany

Although the Cato Journal lists 56 countries that have experienced hyperinflation, we will only look at some of the most significant.

Perhaps the most well-known and the oldest case among the few countries I will review here, is the German Weimar Republic, which experienced a truly dramatic and devastating inflation rate between 1921 and 1923. By 1923, Germany was experiencing a monthly inflation rate of over 29,500%. The value of the German marks, by the end of the year in 1023 was an incredible rate of $1 = 4.2 trillion marks.

In large part, the reason for the incredible inflation rate was a foolish decision on the part of the German government to fund the war related debt resulting from World War One, by borrowing money instead of taxing its citizens or finding a solid means of raising money without insane borrowing. They did eventually find a way to reverse the runaway inflation, but not before many people experienced great hardship.

## Greece

The next country (I am not listing these in any particular order) on the list of nations that have experienced hyperinflation in the last hundred years is Greece. In October 1944 they were experiencing a *monthly* inflation rate of 13,800% (again, that is a thirteen thousand, eight hundred percent inflation in one month. That equates to a daily inflation rate of 20.9%).

World War Two had devastated Greece and left the government in debt. In an attempt to cover its expenses they printed money. Printing money, as discussed above, devalues the already existing money supply. They did this instead of taxing their citizens. Eventually the citizens of

Greece lost faith in the currency. The central bank started issuing gold franc coins, which further cut the demand and value of the currency.

Greece, too, managed to recover from the period of hyperinflation by joining an international concern that linked exchange rates and currencies to the US dollar.

It is interesting that Greece is, once again, facing a crisis in which they no longer have the ability to pay their debt and are essentially robbing the citizens to pay their way.

Although they have linked their economy to the euro, which, of course, Greece cannot just print more of due to the Euro Zone controls and constitution, they currently have to consider dropping out of the Union and establishing their own separate currency, again.

It is not likely to end well… and the cycle continues. After nearly 100 years they are still in financial trouble.

**Yugoslavia**
Yugoslavia went through hyperinflation from 1989 – 1994 during which the monthly inflation rate reached 313,000,000% and the daily inflation rate reached 64.6%. At its worst the bank was printing dinars with denominations as high as 500 billion.

Yugoslavia's inflation was in large part due to printing money. After the UN imposed sanctions on the country there was a sharp drop in output.

By 1990 the government had used up its own hard currency reserves and began to appropriate savings of citizens by restricting access to their savings in government banks.

The country eventually broke-up, which only added to the country's inflation woes. Finally, in 1994, the Yugoslavian government created the *novi dinar*, which they exchanged for the old currency at a rate of one million three hundred thousand dinar to one novi (new) dinar. They then pegged its value to the German mark.

## Zimbabwe

By the end of the 2000 - 2009 hyperinflation period, Zimbabwe was experiencing a staggering annual inflation rate of 516 quintillion percent. That is actually a number that cannot be comprehended by the human mind, much less the wallet.

The National Bank had to start printing Zimbabwean dollars in denominations of 100 trillion so shoppers didn't have to lug around sacks or wheelbarrows of cash.

President Mugabe was directly responsible for much of the inflation. Government spending was financed by the Reserve Bank of Zimbabwe. The nation's inflation rate was a direct result of out of control policies, which involved unrelenting government spending. Naturally, Mugabe blamed US and EU sanctions for the hyperinflation and the resulting economic chaos.

## Argentina (Circa 1980's)

Argentina's experienced an annual inflation rate that hit 12,000% in 1989. The effect of hyperinflation was so severe that one 1983 peso = 100 billion pre-1992 pesos.

Argentina's inflation was the result of a huge emphasis on external borrowing. Since this cannot go on indefinitely, they were cut off from further borrowing. The government devalued the Argentinean currency to increase its trade surplus. That weakened their currency even more.

The government was not without ideas. They tried a variety of things like The Primavera Plan which had a reverse multiple exchange-rate system. This failed. In the 80s it adopted the BB plan with new stabilization measures.

**How it all ended:** Over the years the government tried economic reforms like the above mentioned Primavera Plan and the BB Plan. It is not clear
, to this date, that it has truly ended. Argentina is still implementing measures that are liberal in nature and are threatening the commercial and industrial economy. They are, in fact, trying to repatriate all the money they believe is outside the country.
Not cooperating results in stiff penalties.

## What is coming?

It is pretty clear hyperinflation is not just a western phenomenon. It happens as a result of poor decisions made by governments, regardless of where they are in the world or how modern the society or culture.

The United States has been embracing the notion of spending without regard to funds available. If we are spending more than we have, we just borrow from other countries and pay the interest on both, the tax money collected from the citizens and the money borrowed from those same countries. In other words, we are paying interest on the money we borrow to pay interest.

As if that is not enough, we print money out of thin air to pay this interest. That is no different than writing a check from an account that has no money to pay expenses, and replenishing that money by printing more checks. It does not work for us as individuals and it does not work for the government. If we are honest with ourselves, we have to see that pretty much everything is going up in cost at an unreasonable rate.

If it is not the actual cost of things that is going up, then it is the reduced wages we are receiving to pay for those items. To pay ten dollars for something now with an hourly wage of $10 is a lot harder than paying ten dollars ten years ago with an hourly wage of $20. We deceive ourselves when we find things that have not apparently gone up in cost, but don't pay attention to the reduced ability we have to pay.

The current administration has gone to great lengths to make us think they are responsible for a non-existent economic recovery when there are millions of American citizens who have simply dropped out of the workforce and stopped looking for work.

Once they drop off the official unemployment rolls, the government simply chooses to not count them.

They are no longer among the ranks of the unemployed; no longer a statistic that matters.

The American government is not interested in reducing the budget; because it is the unrestrained spending of money we don't have that supposedly benefits entitlement minded citizens. It was said, 200 years ago, (there is no official record of who said it)

**A true democracy cannot exist as a permanent form of government.**
It can only exist until the voters discover that they can vote themselves largesse from the public treasury. From that moment on, the majority always votes for the candidates promising the most benefits from the public treasury (*does this sound familiar?*) with the result that a democracy always collapses over loose fiscal policy, and it is always followed by a dictatorship.

It is one thing to promise the citizenry services, it is quite another to pay for those services. As it stands, we are nearly a hundred trillion dollars in debt, when one factors in Social Security and Medicare obligations.

That is such an incomprehensible number, it would require the total income of every person in the country for nearly one hundred years to repay. Instead of addressing that issue directly, the government chooses to print more money, thereby reducing the value if the currency and resulting in an increase of the debt The more our money is devalued, the more goods and services will cost and the less likely the countries we owe money to will be to accept our dollars as payment for debt.

Since the value of goods and services are priced in ever diminishing dollars, the less the American public will be willing to accept the same amount of dollars for those goods and services.

We do not need the government to tell us we are experiencing high inflation rates. We can see it in the supermarkets and department stores.

If you don't prepare, now, for the inevitable collapse of the dollar and the rampant resulting inflation, you will certainly suffer the consequences of the poor judgment of the government. There are things that can be done and we will discuss some of those things later in this book.

**Monetary Policy**
Investopedia writes: Following the Federal Reserve Act of 1913, the
Federal Reserve (the U.S. central bank) was given the authority to formulate U.S. monetary policy. To do this, the Federal Reserve uses three tools:
*open market operations, the discount rate and reserve requirements.*

Wikipedia writes: "Monetary policy concerns the actions of a central bank or other regulatory authorities that determine the size and rate of growth of the money supply. In the United States, the Federal Reserve is in charge of monetary policy, and implements it primarily by performing operations that influence short-term interest rates.
It goes on to say: "The Federal Reserve has three main mechanisms for manipulating the money supply. It can buy or sell treasury securities.
Selling securities has the effect of reducing the monetary base (because it accepts money in return for purchase of securities), taking that money out of circulation.

Purchasing treasury securities increases the monetary base (because it pays out hard currency in exchange for accepting securities). Secondly, the discount rate can be changed. And finally, the Federal Reserve can adjust the reserve requirement [for banks], which can affect the money multiplier; the reserve requirement is adjusted only infrequently, and was last adjusted in 1992."

*G. Edward Griffin,* in his book *"The Creature of Jekyll Island,"* says his definition of money is:
"...anything that is accepted as a medium of exchange and it may be classified into the following forms:

*1. Commodity money* (money whose value comes from a commodity of which it is made. Commodity money consists of objects that have value in themselves as well as value in their use as money.
Examples of commodities that have been used as mediums of exchange include gold, silver, copper, salt, etc.)

*2. Receipt money* (In the beginning, banks served as warehouses for the safe keeping of their customers' coins. When they issued paper receipts for those coins, they converted commodity money into receipt money.

This was a great convenience, but it did not alter the money supply. People had a choice of using either coin or paper but they could not use both. If they used coin, the receipt was never issued. If they used the receipt, the coin remained in the vault and did not circulate.

When the banks abandoned this practice and began to issue receipts to borrowers, they became magicians. Some have said they created money out of nothing, but that is not quite true. What they did was even more amazing. They created money out of debt.)

*3. Fiat money* (American Heritage dictionary. Paper money decreed legal tender ... not backed by gold or silver.)

*4. Fractional money* (Fractional money is defined as paper money with precious-metal backing for part, not all of its stated value...

Fractional money always degenerates into pure fiat money.) He began defining the varying roles or characteristics of money after the acting Treasurer, *M. E. Slindee,* responded to an individual asking for

five dollars of lawful money in exchange for the five dollar Federal Reserve Note he sent in to them, by saying, "You are advised that the term 'Lawful Money' has not been defined in Federal legislation," whereupon they returned his $5 Federal Reserve Note.

In that chapter dealing with the definition of money, Griffin goes on to explaining, to a very definite degree, what money is and how the Federal Reserve controls and uses it.

It does not take a rocket scientist to know the Federal Reserve controls virtually every aspect of monetary policy. It tries to control inflation by raising and lowering interest rates.

At the *Foundationforliving.org,* they express it this way: *The Fed is* trying to maintain a "healthy" economy. If the economy is "very slow" the Fed might decide to lower interest rates that will in turn make money more available to businesses, home buyers, and consumers. If the economy is "heating up" *and in the opinion of the Fed -- growing too quickly,* they will raise interest rates to "slow things down".

Over the past several years, the Federal Reserve has used this methodology in ever increasing extremes.

*Quantitative Easing* has been one of those ways. The Feds "print" paperless money by the billions and use it to purchase bonds.

Over the years since around 2010, they have flooded the market with about four trillion dollars, which actually never existed, but is meant to stimulate the economy. Since it is only money in the minds of those who obediently accept it as money, it serves to increase the amount of money that is put into an otherwise stagnant stock market.

Once created, whether real or not, it never goes away. The Feds now own the bonds they purchased with fiat money and can presumably sell them for "real money" (albeit fiat) at any time in the future. That increases the Fed's bottom line, but has not created anything of real value.

It is such policies that lead to the crisis we see in Greece and other EU countries that are on the verge of bankruptcy. The only way the United
States Government could realistically expunge the huge debt it has incurred would be to declare bankruptcy. It would destroy the credit of our government, but it would put us back on a path of manageable monetary policy.

Since gold and silver have historically always been a medium of exchange, it would make sense to purchase some amount of either or both to provide you with a hedge against hyperinflation. While paper (fiat) money might become completely worthless in the eyes of the population, ***there has never been a time in history when gold or silver did not have value.***

In fact, gold might be worth around $1260 per ounce, at the time of this writing, but the less value paper money has, the more value an ounce of gold would have against the reduced value of the currency.

It is unlikely comparing the reduced dollar to another currency (like the $1 = 4.2 Trillion Marks rate during the Weimar Regime, in Germany) would have any real meaning or value. Instead, it is likely an ounce of gold would be worth $10,000 or $100,000 or $1,000,000. In purchasing power, the value would not likely have changed a whole lot although the perceived value could be a lot more.

A five dollar loaf of bread is currently about one two hundred fortieth of an ounce of gold. If an ounce of gold is worth $1,000,000 and a loaf of bread is $4,166, it is still 1/240 of an ounce of gold. Your buying potential has not gone down. If anything, those receiving the gold are going to be more inclined to give you a better exchange rate, because they are receiving something much more substantial and with intrinsic value than paper in exchange for that loaf of bread.

**The Mark of the beast**
Times have changed, significantly, over the last hundred years. In Argentina and Greece, monetary problems are still being dealt with in a pretty much traditional way.

Banks restrict the withdrawal of cash to a certain amount, either per day or per month. Credit cards are used to pay "money" to others for goods and services, but it is still money that has value according to the current economic conditions.

It costs money to print money. Whether the government prints five dollar bills, hundred dollar bills, million dollar bills, or trillion dollar bills, there is a real cost involved. One has to have paper (and the US dollar paper is not simple or cheap), ink, printing presses, etc., to generate paper money.

In today's technological age, it is not difficult to imagine the "dollars" as digital numbers that relate to an account at a financial institution, like a bank, and the means of spending that money being a card, a chip, or a scan-able number tattooed on your forearm, wrist, forehead, or any other convenient appendage.

None of the imaginable means of storing or spending "money," discussed above, will impact on the value of money. If the dollar is a number on an account statement or a paper money bill, it will be equally valuable or worthless.

Refusing to take part in the particular form of monetary exchange will only make things more difficult to acquire or sell. The only alternative will, again, be a medium of exchange that is *outside that system* that virtually everyone will accept and recognize.

If you think the requirements of a digital system of currency are too complex and burdensome to be realistic, just imagine the complexity of monitoring every phone call or email generated in a single day in the United States. That, by itself, seems like an impossibility, yet the NSA is doing exactly that.

When Hillary Clinton says she can no longer supply copies of her emails to the oversight committee, she may in fact not have the ability (not to mention the intent) to do so.

The NSA, however, has already recorded every one of the emails she has sent or received in their data banks. For the NSA to search and find the emails, at the speed of electronics, it would only take a matter of moments to pull them up. *Can we really doubt that?*

When I type a search parameter into Google's search engine, like "how many emails," it takes .59 seconds (less than a second) to come up with 689,000,000 results.

Putting a more specific parameter into NSA's database, like Hillary Clinton, would probably not take a minute to read, select, and gather all her emails into one file. That data would include those emails she sent as well as those she received.

If one tried to imagine a paper filing system to keep track of all the letters and phone transcriptions being saved every day, the size of the facility would have to be as large as a small state. The reduction in size by doing everything digitally has reduced that physical requirement to a large building in Utah.

As miniaturization has become more advanced, it is not inconceivable to believe that same facility could house all the information on every person and business in the country, including banking and other financial information.

Since a number of eighteen digits (presumably the number of digits in a number that has six + six + six digits) has more than enough combinations to number everyone in the world a couple times over, it is conceivable the Biblical *"Mark-of- The-Beast"* could be a chip under the skin which identifies you as you walk by any "reader" in the vicinity.

It would automatically deduct monetary amounts from accounts that are related to the number on the chip. It would make it impossible to purchase anything from a conventional outlet without having them identify who you are and whether you have enough "money" to purchase the item(s). It would give police the ability to immediately identify you, determine your criminal background and provide an immediate medical history.

In order to live outside such a system, it would be required to find things of value to barter with. One might trade or barter a silver coin for several shovels. One could then trade a shovel for a certain amount of produce or meat from a farmer; all under the table, of course.

The farmer could then use the shovel to grow more produce, which he could then trade for seeds. We would have, effectively, reverted back to *the original monetary system* in order to avoid the all invasive and worthless monetary system of our government.

It is, of course, the western world that is providing the technological advancements that create a foundation for such a system. So the answer to the original question, "Is western civilization the cause or the cure?" is both *yes and no*. It is western civilization that could be providing the means to usher in the Mark-of-the-Beast (which will, by the way, not be confined to America since it will be a means of controlling any citizenry). It is, however, every country with an out of control government that is ripe for hyperinflation.

# Can We Trust Banks?

## Why Do We Put Our Money in Banks?

Are banks a necessary evil? If we don't put our money in a bank, how do we do any kind of transaction? We generally put our paycheck into the bank so we can write checks to purchase things.

As a middle man, many banks offer credit card services so we can pay for those things we need or want without having to carry too much cash, and then pay the banks to reimburse those amounts paid by the card. But where did the concept of banks come from?

Banking goes back as far as 400 years B.C. although not in its current form.

For our purposes, we will look at the 1800s, starting with the Rothschild family. That family got involved in international banking in the middle of the 1800s.

The banks, for the last few hundred years, were set up for a variety of reasons from holding deposits and valuables, to lending money (often at more than 12% and up to 45% interest per annum), and to financing governments who needed to fund their wars.

They were also set up to be able to accept money from a payor and write up a check that would then be accepted by other banks. One could also pay a debt by depositing the money into one bank and have it considered paid by another. That removed the need to physically transport money to another city, state, or country, which was always a risky business.

Throughout history, banks have been huge money-making propositions. Many wealthy people and families were created in banking, but a lot of those fortunes were short lived. Royalty and regimes that borrowed large sums of money were prone to defaulting on those loans, which bankrupted many of the bankers.

Nevertheless, the banking business was lucrative enough to entice more families into that sector.

Today we are compelled by both training and pragmatism to put our money in banks for a variety of reasons and banks exist for a variety of incredibly good financial reasons. For customers the advantages are:

- Safety (because of banks, you don't have to store money in your house or carry it on you waiting to be robbed)
- Ability to store your money in an instrument or account that will pay interest (although it is almost non-existent today)
- Ability to pay for goods and services by writing a check
- To finance the purchase of a car
- To finance the purchase of a home, business, commercial property
- To invest in CDs and T-bills and other investment vehicles.

The irony is, the amount banks are paying in interest is far and away less than the current rate of inflation. That means you are losing money if you have money in the bank.

There are banks in Europe, right now, where you, the depositor, actually have to pay interest (usually expressed as a negative interest) to the bank for the privilege of leaving your money in their care.

I don't know about you, but the idea of paying a bank to hold my money, and use it for their benefit (they invest and lend the deposits and earn interest on that money), simply doesn't make sense to me.
Although there are still conveniences one derives from banking, much of the stated and implied benefits of banking are no longer applicable.

My wife recently had to withdraw $5,000 from our bank to pay for something we purchased. Although there was far more in the account than was needed to cover the withdrawal, the teller had to get the manager and they spent several minutes in conference, pointing and gesticulating at the computer screen before they finally came back to my wife and with an apparent degree of reluctance and decided to let her have the money.

If you use more than a few thousand dollars of your own funds, the banks are now required to file a **Suspicious Activity Report (SAR).** It makes no difference that it is your money in the account or that it has been duly deposited, and seasoned in the account, or that you present the tellers with proof you are doing a legitimate transaction, they are required to file a SAR simply because, in the government's view, no normal citizen would have need of so much money for any legitimate purpose in every-day life.

My wife said they made her feel like a criminal. *"They don't have a problem when I deposit money, why do they make it so difficult to withdraw the money?"* she asked when she got home. It would not be too difficult to imagine an American Citizen no longer being allowed to withdraw more than a certain amount each month. That is exactly what the situation is in Greece, at the time I am writing this.

Although it is getting to be more and more difficult, many of the wealthy, and even the not-so-wealthy, are starting to move their cash to banks overseas. Even though America has a great deal of authority over global banks, which makes it more difficult to open an account in banks in other countries, it is legal and makes it much more difficult for the US government to block or close overseas accounts.

*Opening an account in a bank in Singapore, Hong Kong, Belize, Cook Islands, and several*
*other countries is still possible.* If you sign up for Simon Black's "Sovereign Man" (www.sovereignman.com), newsletter or Doug Casey's "International Man" (www.internationalman.com), newsletter, they often talk about which foreign banks still do business
with Americans, as well as giving very researched and sound advice on how to protect yourself against financial ruin and tyranny.

**The Rothschild legacy**

The name, "Rothschild," is well known in the banking industry and most everyone in America has heard the name, in context with banking, at one time or another. What is probably not well known is the context that name has in how the banking industry is controlling and destroying America's way of life.

The Rothschild family, which started in the mid-1800's with *Mayer Amschel Rothschild*, who was quoted as saying: *"Let me issue and control a nation's money and I care not who writes the laws,"*

His original family name was *Bauer*, but after his father's death, in Frankfurt, Germany, he decided to change his name to Rothschild. There was a red shield hanging over the door of his villa with a picture of an eagle. Red shield in German is ***Rot[es] Schild***. He added five arrows to be held in one of the eagle's feet to symbolize his five sons.

Although not a banker in the same sense as bankers are known today, a discussion on banks must eventually come to the discussion of the Rothschild family. In those days, bankers did not take individual's deposits and reinvest it as banks do today. The bankers of that era were primarily wealthy individuals who would lend their own money to people or governments who were already wealthy and did not mind paying very high interest rates on the money borrowed.

The Rothschilds were often instrumental in financing both sides of the wars that were raging in Europe. War was such a financially beneficial enterprise for the Rothschilds; they encouraged the various governments to enter into a conflict and then offered to finance that conflict.

Continuing down in history, the father and sons were all involved in financing wars including historically well known, from funding the opponents of Napoleon on behalf of the governments of England, France, Prussia, Austria, and Belgium, to funding the governments of Spain, Naples, Portugal, Brazil, various German states, and other smaller countries. They were the personal bankers of many of the crowned heads of Europe. They made large investments, through agents, in markets as distant as the United States, India, Cuba, and Australia.

According to Biographer Derek Wilson:
*"Those who lampooned or vilified the Rothschilds for their 'sinister' influence had a considerable amount of justification for their anger and anxiety. The banking community had always constituted a 'fifth estate' whose members were able, by their control of royal purse strings, to affect important events.*

*But the house of Rothschild was immensely more powerful than any financial empire that had ever preceded it. It commanded vast wealth. It was international. It was independent. Royal governments were nervous of it because they could not control it.*

*Popular movements hated it because it was not answerable to the people.*
*Constitutionalists resented it because its influence was exercised behind the scenes—secretly."*

Often, the Rothschilds were less concerned about the interest rates they charged than with the privileges and immunities granted them by the governments they did business with. This immunity allowed them to deal in a thriving black market for cotton goods, yams, tobacco, coffee, sugar, and indigo; and they moved freely through the borders of Germany, Scandinavia, Holland, Spain, England, and France. This government protection was one of those indirect benefits that generated commercial profits far in excess of the interest received on the underlying government loans.

They were also granted the rights to things like mining of minerals. There was no end to the ways the Rothschild family was able to profit richly from their less than moral or honorable business tactics.

Once again, G. Edward Griffin, in his book, "The Creature Of Jekyll Island," expresses the manner in which the Rothschilds conducted business as *"THE FORMULA."* He expressed that formula as follows:

"Let us imagine a man who is totally pragmatic. He is smarter and more cunning than most men and, in fact, holds them in thinly disguised contempt. He may respect the talents of a few, but has little concern over the condition of mankind.

He has observed that kings and politicians are always fighting over something or other and has concluded that wars are inevitable. He also has learned that wars can be profitable, not only by lending or creating the money to finance them, but from government favoritism in the granting of commercial subsidies or monopolies.

He is not capable of such a primitive feeling as patriotism, so he is free to participate in the funding of any side in any conflict, limited only by factors of self-interest. If such a man were to survey the world around him, it is not difficult to imagine that he would come to the following conclusions which would become the prime directives of his career:

*1. War is the ultimate discipline to any government.* If it can successfully meet the challenge of war, it will survive. If it cannot, it will perish. All else is secondary.

The sanctity of its laws, the prosperity of its citizens, and the solvency of its treasury will be quickly sacrificed by any government in its primal act of self-survival.

*2. All that is necessary, therefore, to insure that a government will maintain or expand its debt is to involve it in war or the threat of war.*

The greater the threat and the more destructive the war, the greater the need for debt.

*3. To involve a country in war or the threat of war, it will be necessary for it to have enemies with credible military might.*

If such enemies already exist, all the better. If they exist but lack military strength, it will be necessary to provide them the money to build their war machine. If an enemy does not exist at all, then it will be necessary to create one by financing the rise of a hostile regime.

*4. The ultimate obstacle is a government which declines to finance its wars through debt.*

Although this seldom happens, when it does, it will be necessary to encourage internal political opposition, insurrection, or revolution to replace that government with one that is more compliant to our will. The assassination of heads of state could play an important role in this process.

*5. No nation can be allowed to remain militarily stronger than its adversaries*, for that could lead to peace and a reduction of debt. To accomplish this balance of power, it may be necessary to finance both sides of the conflict.

Unless one of the combatants is hostile to our interests and, therefore, must be destroyed, neither side should be allowed a decisive victory or defeat. While we must always proclaim the virtues of peace, *the unspoken objective is perpetual war*."

Although Griffin admits none of that formula was never expressed *as such* and was certainly never voiced or written down as a formula, it was certainly followed in the way bankers did business in those times.

If you look at what is going on with the lenders in the various countries, today, you can see that banks of those countries lend money to countries to promote war, conflict, and the favors of governments, and gain interest, privilege, and the granting of commercial subsidies and markets.

One can see that in the benefits currently being enjoyed by governments like China, Japan, and other countries that are experiencing great profit in selling their wares in our country. In return, the banks in our country are profiting by lending money to the American economy to finance the import of the products of other countries.

In the early 1900s, JP Morgan slipped into the role so effectively put into motion by the Rothschilds. Morgan was financing all sides of the WW-II conflict and, even at that time, to the tune of billions of dollars. They had effectively cornered the market during that war.

In fact, it is pretty clear the US entered the war for the explicit purpose of protecting the interest of the banks (especially JP Morgan) and their loans to the foreign governments which were funding the war.
The Bank of the United States was a predecessor to the Federal Reserve

Bank. Andrew Jackson, who waged a moral and political war against the Bank of the United States, said in 1829, *"Is there no danger to our liberty and independence in a bank that in its nature has so little to bind it to our country?... [Is there not] cause to tremble for the purity of our elections in peace and for the independence of our country in war?...*

*Controlling our currency, receiving our public monies, and holding thousands of our citizens in dependence, it would be more formidable and dangerous than a naval or military power…"*

The enemy Creature of Jekyll Island is instructive and I would rate it high on your list of important books to read. It covers this topic much more thoroughly than I can, here.
(**http://bit.do/bookclub100**)

Important to know is that the Federal
Reserve is a culmination of the influence and control exercised by
the bankers we have discussed.

Wikipedia says:
"The Federal Reserve
System (also known as the Federal Reserve, or more informally as
*the Fed*) is the central banking system of the United States. It was
created on December 23, 1913, with the enactment of the Federal
Reserve Act, largely in response to a series of financial panics,
particularly a severe panic in 1907.

Over time, the roles and responsibilities of the Federal Reserve
System have expanded, and its structure has evolved. Events such
as the Great Depression in the 1930s were major factors leading to
changes in the system.

The U.S. Congress established three key objectives for monetary
policy in the Federal Reserve Act: Maximum employment, stable
prices, and moderate long-term interest rates."

As such, we can see that Andrew Jackson (7th president of the US)
was right. What we are witnessing in today's news, the
perpetuation of racial unrest, perpetuation of wars, economic
disintegration, political intimidation, and more, is the result of the
need for bankers to be in control and make money, regardless of
the cost to the nation or it's citizens.

*The Federal Reserve Bank has never been audited.* It seems to
operate outside both the normal parameters of corporations or
banks and the controls of Congress.

We would do well to end the reign of terror from the Federal
Reserve Bank. In the meantime, however, we need to make plans
to find a different medium for currency if we wish to preserve our
wealth regardless of what level of wealth you have.

**Jekyll Island**
In 1910 there came together, under the strictest of secrecy, a group of men who met on Jekyll Island representing *fully one fourth of the wealth of the entire world*.

The secrecy and security was unmatched in any previous event, including preparations for war. It was not for recreation that ¼ of the world's wealth was represented in this meeting. It was to come to an agreement on the structure and operation of a banking cartel.

The goal of the cartel, as is true with all cartels, was to maximize profits by minimizing competition between members, to make it difficult for new competitors to enter the field, and to utilize the police power of government to enforce the cartel agreement.

In more specific terms, the purpose and, indeed, the actual outcome of this meeting was to create the blueprint for the Federal Reserve System.
This group of wealthy representatives was from the major nations of the world and they were the men of which Griffin wrote, "The composition of the Jekyll Island meeting was a classic example of cartel structure.

A cartel is a group of independent businesses which join together to coordinate the production, pricing, or marketing of their members. The purpose of a cartel is to reduce competition and thereby increase profitability.

This is accomplished through a shared monopoly over their industry which forces the public to pay higher prices for their goods or services than would be otherwise required under free-enterprise competition."

That cartel continues, today. With the power to create money out of thin air, they wield extreme control over government, business entities, banks, and the average man. Although there are currently governments who are stepping up to the plate to unseat the very controlling giants that exercise that control, it is pretty obvious to those with eyes open, new cartels will occupy that same space that is created by the waning cartel.

That change is being brought about by the increasing greed and control the American government and the current cartel are pushing onto the banks in other countries. It is that very pushy nature of the current administration to force the banks of other countries to follow their rules and laws that is making it difficult to find an international bank that will accept Americans as customers.

# Move Your Money Out Of Banks And Out Of Harm's Way

## Greece Sets the Standard

In the past several years, Greece has frequently been in the news. The worldwide recession brought Greece to its economic knees. Although they can no longer print money, as a member of the European Union, they have done things that we can fully expect to have happen in our own country when we get to the point that the dollar is no longer the reserve currency.

Greece made headlines when it issued decrees saying their citizens can no longer withdraw more than 1,000 euros per month (and, as of this week have declared a bank "holiday" preventing their citizens from getting more than 50 euros per day from ATMs).

They are no longer allowed to export their own money to other countries. The people continue to demand the government take care of them and the government is more than happy to be seen, by their citizens, as their benefactor. The Government refuses to reduce its spending thereby taking steps of austerity, saying that to do so would "hurt" the very people who count on them. They are asking for more and more "loans" from the EU, but any tendency from the EU to bail them out, again and again, usually meets with threats of veto by Germany.

The Greek government, rather than being contrite, assumes an attitude as though it deserves to be kept afloat, even though it is not willing to do what it needs to in order to help itself.

Right now we can print money out of thin air and other countries continue to accept it as payment, even though it has less and less value.

That is because of the role of the US dollar as the reserve currency. As you will see, there are many other countries that are actively plotting and acting on the idea of replacing the current reserve currency with the Chinese yuan. Will that be any better? That depends on what you consider better. Why won't a more international currency assume the role of reserve currency? It is fairly evident the euro is in as bad or worse shape than the dollar. One can see that the euro is declining in value in relationship to and faster than the dollar.

Politicians believe they are doing the right things to shore up the dollar and that they are responsible for a stronger dollar. Since there is invariably a reserve currency, most countries do not care which currency it is.

They will have to purchase and sell in that currency, whichever it is, and there will be no significant advantage to having one over the other.
That is probably true for all but the country which has the reserve currency.

What we are seeing in Greece is not unique. We have seen similar and equally futile steps being taken in other countries, from Argentina to
Poland, to Italy, and Ireland. The only difference between those countries and the US is that we happen to be the current kingpin and have the ability to print more fiat money at will.

The Federal Reserve has spent the last four years printing money to purchase unwanted or otherwise unsellable bonds. Quantitative Easing has been used to create (*Again, out of thin air*) about *four trillion dollars*. That has watered down the value of the dollar enormously.

Fortunately, or perhaps unfortunately, the Swiss-franc, British pound, euro, and pretty much every other major currency, has declined in value as much or more than the dollar.

America has already set into motion the necessary restrictions and laws to prevent the dollar from being easily exported. While it is not actually illegal to take money with you to other countries, it has been in effect for a while that one must disclose whether one is taking *more than $10,000 per family* with them out of the country.

Wiring money to overseas accounts is getting more and more difficult. There are reporting requirements for those who have money in overseas accounts. If one has more than a certain (and potentially ever changing) amount in one or more accounts (*aggregate*), one is required to file an FBAR (Foreign Bank Account Report) as well as a FATCA (Foreign Account Tax Compliance Act) form, every year, disclosing what the maximum amounts of those accounts were for that year.

"This is a piece of legislation that is so big and so far-reaching, and [has] so many different moving pieces, and is rolling out in an incremental fashion . . . that you really won't be able to know what its consequences are, intended or otherwise," said US National Tax Advocate Nina Olsen.

The consequences of making the filings mandatory and a criminal offense, if not adhered to, are not only overwhelming for the tax payer, but very costly for foreign banks doing business with Americans.

There are many people who are Americans by accident of birth. They are either born to foreigners who were briefly in America, born to Americans in another country, or to Americans who have immigrated to another country and subsequently had children. Most are not aware of an obligation to file taxes with the US. Nevertheless, they become criminals if they do not comply with the long arm of US law.

*The United States of America is one of only two governments that tax its citizens no matter where they are in the world.*

The other country is Eritrea, a small country by Ethiopia. The American representative to the United Nations joined in criticism of the country of Eritrea for taxing its citizens a 2% income tax, regardless of where they are in the world or where their income is derived.

In 2011, the United Nations identified this 2% tax on Eritrean nationals living overseas as unacceptable and the UN Security Council passed resolution 2023 condemning the Eritrean government for imposing a tax on non-resident citizens.

The resolution says, "Eritrea shall cease using extortion, threats of violence, fraud and other illicit means to collect taxes outside of Eritrea from its nationals or other individuals of Eritrean descent." The United Nations found the 2% tax to be so invasive, it had to pass a Resolution to try to stop it.

Unbelievably, the United States of America voted *for the resolution*; even though the USA is guilty of exactly the same kind of taxation, only at a much higher percentage (15-40%).

The IRS is, for instance, demanding taxes from the mayor of London, who was born in America, which gives him automatic citizenship, even though he has not lived in America since he was 5 years old. Because of his political office, he is unlikely to have to pay up, but those who are not political celebrities do not enjoy that same protection.

The long and short of it is, we are following in Greece's footsteps. It will not be long, at the rate the US is going, before we will not be able to access the money in our own bank accounts. It will not be long before the US will charge a wealth or asset tax on monies and assets in our possession, perhaps as much as a 10% tax, just for the privilege of living, whether proudly or unknowingly, as a US citizen.

*The die is cast.*
*We will either find a way to exclude ourselves from the coming tyranny and financial meltdown, or we will suffer under it*.

**Can Bail-Outs Protect Your Deposits?**
President Franklin D. Roosevelt signed the Social Security Act into law on August 14, 1935 at 3:30 p.m. The new law was ostensibly to help those who were otherwise not in the right mind to plan for old age.

At the time, it was assumed most people would not live to see their 65th birthday and therefore the money they paid in would remain in the social security trust fund, making it self-sufficient and was thought to be without much risk.

The act, which was amended in 1939, established a number of programs designed to provide aid to various segments of the population.
Unemployment compensation and AFDC (originally Aid to Dependent Children) are two of the programs that still exist today.

A number of government agencies were created to oversee the welfare programs. Some of the agencies that deal with welfare in the United States are the Department of Health and Human Services (HHS), the Department of Housing and Urban Development (HUD), the Department of Labor, the Department of Agriculture, and the Department of Education.

Welfare history continued to be made in 1996 when President Bill Clinton signed the Personal Responsibility and Work Opportunity

Reconciliation Act. Under the act, the federal government gives annual lump sums to the states to use to assist the poor.

In turn, the states must adhere to certain criteria to ensure that those receiving aid are being encouraged to move from welfare to work. Though some have criticized the program, many acknowledge it has been successful.
**([www.welfareinfo.org/history](www.welfareinfo.org/history))**

We can acknowledge the need to help individuals who are suffering illness, disability, or financial distress. In the case of Social Security, it is a form of help to those who have paid into the system and receive back what they have paid in.

In the case of welfare, it is a social contract pretty much everyone feels is justifiable, assuming it is not abused by the recipient or the agency paying it out. What seems less justified is large corporations, who have, for the most part, been making bad decisions that cause a state of bankruptcy.

When the economy took a nose-dive in 2007 and later, the insurance giants started crying foul and demanded the US government give them billions of dollars from the American tax payers to help them get back on their feet again.

Banks that had been making sub-prime loans to individuals who could not possibly pay back their mortgages, soon found themselves in deep water when they had to start foreclosing on these properties. They knew the borrower would not be able to pay.

They had qualified under very loose guidelines and under adjustable rates that often included negative amortization; that is to say a loan that increased in amount each month, because the monthly payment did not even cover the interest. It was clear the borrower would be further under water once the rate adjusted to a higher amount.

***Barney Franks and Chris Dodd*** had created legislation and bullied banks into making unsound loans so those unfortunate enough to not qualify for the "American Dream", could now experience home ownership.

Banks, unfortunately, were far too willing to pocket the commissions for each new or refinanced loan. It did not seem to matter that the borrower would be assured of only temporary ownership and a certain foreclosure.

I, personally, knew a woman who had refinanced her house to pay for some repairs. She had originally owed $129,000 and refinanced the house for $300,000. She was on a fixed income of $1,500 per month, but somehow she was approved for a loan on a house that was not close to being worth and a monthly payment of nearly $3,000. She was in foreclosure within three months of refinancing, but the bank had earned nearly $10,000 on the loan.

Perhaps the woman should have suffered the consequences of making an unintelligent decision, but should the bank have been rewarded by being bailed out for making bad loans?

To make matters worse, banks that had been responsible and did not practice the subprime lending game were forced to take some of the bail-out money and pay it back with interest.

None of this was voted on by the American voters. None of it made any sense. Even car manufacturers who allowed the cost of manufacturing cars to be far greater than their foreign competitors managed to get into the corporate welfare game.

It can be argued that those corporations that took the corporate welfare money have bounced back, to some degree, and that warranted the payment of those monies to them. Far more logically, it would have been both more constructive and educational for the corporations that were near bankruptcy, whether banks, insurance companies, or car manufacturers, to be forced by their own incompetence to go through bankruptcy and either fail completely or to rise from the ashes.

Yes, a lot of people would have lost their jobs, but what did we see instead?
Corporations and CEOs made a killing, downsized, and laid people off. The unemployment rate skyrocketed as a result of the cutbacks. People lost their homes, and have had to go on unemployment and/or welfare.

The economy is worse than ever, but at least the fat cats in the corporations have done all right for themselves. I am not *anti-corporation*, I just believe their consequence should have been bankruptcy, rather than bailouts.

Obviously, bailouts were and are not the answer. Only extreme liberals, who think throwing money you don't have at the problems is the answer, feel good about it. Actual unemployment is far higher than the left wing media and government are willing to admit. People who have dropped off the unemployment rolls, because they no longer qualify for unemployment, have basically dropped out of the workforce.

They are no longer counted among the unemployed. Large numbers of those people have started collecting disability. Not able to find a job or collect unemployment, getting money under social security disability extends their ability to survive without employment.

Either way, it is a huge drain on the economy. Either way the government continues to think it can spend its way out of the recession. Bailouts not only don't help the banks, they don't help you out, either.

Just as welfare is not the answer for those who don't have a self-generated source of income, corporate welfare only makes the banks and large corporations lazy and perpetuate their comfort level in relying on an outside agency to pick up the pieces when they fall.


**Why Not Just Print More Money?**
An online publication, known as *Economics and Liberty*, says the following:
In actuality, the best approach is to let the people (the free market) decide what they want to use as money. There is no need for a central bank, government control, or legal tender laws.

History has shown that, when left up to the people, silver and gold tend to gravitate to the role of money for the following reasons:
1. *scarcity* – supply cannot be manipulated like fiat money which causes the boom and bust cycles in the economy
2. *durability* – gold and silver will not rot, burn, or deteriorate, which makes them a great store of value
3. *fungible and divisible* – they can be divided into small, interchangeable amounts which make them ideal for trade.
4. *portable* – Their high concentration of value allows you to carry and store substantial value
5. *proven* – gold and silver have been used as money for over 6000 years of recorded history.
6. *use value* – both gold and silver have tremendous use value in industry. The highest use value though is in their role as money.

Anyone who has purchased Gold recognizes its intrinsic value. The same is true of silver, but to a lesser degree. Governments have generally acknowledged the intrinsic value of these precious metals by striking coins of various values from them.

Gold and silver, both, are usually denominated in ounces and fractions of ounces. Originally in
America, one ounce of silver was valued at one dollar. Thus silver dollars contain one ounce of actual silver. Since they are alloyed with other metals to make them more durable, the actual weight of the silver dollar is slightly more than one ounce, which is to insure there is actually one ounce of silver.

For much of our early history, Silver coins were denominated in smaller fractions of an ounce. A dime, for instance, was 1/10th of an ounce, a quarter was ¼ of an ounce, and a fifty cent piece (or half dollar) was ½ of an ounce of silver.

One of the things people do today as a hedge against the total devaluation of the dollar, is to purchase what is commonly referred to as *"junk" silver*. In today's market a $1000 face value bag of pre-1965 silver coins (with a worn coin weight of about 715 troy ounces) has a dollar value of about $13,225.

While this kind of purchase is not generally considered an investment that depends on increased value over time, it is indeed going to increase in value if the spot price of silver increases.

Many people purchase these bags of junk coins as a hedge against the crash of the paper dollar.
If and (*I believe*) when that happens, the value of gold and silver will increase, dramatically. It will be far more practical, if silver goes to $200 per ounce, to be able to pay for things with dimes (1/10 ounce of silver), which will have an equivalent value of $20.

On the other hand, one ounce of gold, as a coin, was originally struck as a twenty dollar coin. Today, the government is still in the business of making $20 gold pieces, which are one ounce, but the actual value is determined by the current price of gold, plus any numismatic value the coin might have.

One ounce of gold at the time of this writing hovers around $1,200. Paper money, of course, has no intrinsic value.

It is the communal belief in the value of paper money that gives it the ability to be exchanged for a commodity or service, which does have intrinsic value.

Let's say, hypothetically, that we have a total amount of paper money in circulation of around $1,000,000,000 (one billion dollars). Let us also assume we have a total value of goods and services of $1,000,000,000.

If that were the case, there would be a balance of money to goods and services. Originally, each dollar was backed by gold or silver in the possession of the treasury.

Once we went off the gold and silver standard, the value of the dollar was substantiated by our belief that the federal government would stand behind the currency.

Regardless of the real value of money in balance with goods and services, when new money is printed without increasing the amount of goods and services and without having something of value backing the paper money then the balance of money to goods and services gets skewed. The more money there is in circulation, the more out of balance things get.

More money means less value. If the amount of paper money increases to $2,000,000,000, and the amount of goods and services remain the same, the money is worth only half what it used to be.

Obviously, the example assumes the increase in money supply without an increase in goods and services. It is not quite than simple or straight forward, but you get the idea. The Federal Reserve has increased the money supply, in the last five years, by as much as four trillion Dollars.

There has been no corresponding increase in goods and services (Gross Domestic Product) in those five years. In fact, if anything the GDP has decreased. At some point, the other nations will understandably start saying they don't want to retain the dollar as reserve currency, because they know each dollar is being devalued by the increase in the money supply.

Russia and China are both making it clear, right now, they are not interested in retaining the dollar-valued bonds and assets they currently have. They are divesting themselves of their dollars and buying more gold. That speaks volumes as to the direction the dollar is headed and the importance of having precious metals.

**So to review**, printing money is increasing the number of paper notes in circulation, but does nothing, in the long run, toward stabilizing the economy. $10 in today's dollars may purchase what $.50 to $1.00 purchased ten or fifteen years ago. That comes out to *an inflation rate of between 6% and 10% per year*.

Both the second decade of the 1900s and the 1970s had very large annual inflation rates. Beginning in 1913, inflation averaged about 10% per year and in the 1970s the averaged inflation rate was just over 7% a year. T

his resulted in a cumulative total inflation for the years 1913 (When the Federal Reserve was formed and started tracking inflation) until the end of 1919 of 97.96% (less than a decade) and the inflationary 1970's saw 102.91% over the entire decade.

Against the 7% average rate of inflation in the 1970's, which we would consider terrible, the 2% or 3% per year since 1990 might not sound so bad.

However, the total cumulative inflation for the nearly 22 years from January 1990 through September 2012 is 81.64%. In other words, something that cost $100 in January of 1990 would cost $181.64 in September of 2012 and this is what happens at "low" inflation rates.

The thing most people are not aware of is that the government seldom reports the actual numbers. They are more likely to stick to real numbers for historical data, dating back before their influence, but the numbers they release for the term they are in charge of are most often adjusted by some means to make the current administration look better.

# Take Charge Of Your 401-K
# & Other Retirement Accounts

## Who Owns Your Money?

On the face of it, that sounds like an odd question, doesn't it? Yet it is the most obvious question to ask about money that says "Federal Reserve Note" on the face of the bill. It is money given to you with an obligation tied to it; a debt owed to you by the Federal Reserve.

You may be in possession of a monetary note, and that possession gives you the opportunity, if not the right, to trade that note for a commodity of service. That does not, however, mean you own that note.

The Federal Reserve can demand return of that note at any time. Of course they will not, because that note has no value to them, either. Nor does it obligate them absolutely to pay on that note.

That fact alone underscores the point that we have built a "house of cards." The only thing holding this house of cards up is the tenuous belief the population, at large, has in the system. We have been effectively indoctrinated, over the last hundred years, to have faith that the American Government backs up the value of our money.

It is when people start losing that belief, that the system will start its dramatic decline (although in reality it already has begun).

The paper money system has not been called *fiat currency* for no reason. This is not just applicable to the US dollar. The Japanese yen, for example, carries unfathomable denominations.

One dollar equals approximately 119 yen, as of April 29, 2015. That means $100 is almost 12,000 yen. It requires almost 610 Chilean pesos to make one dollar. That means it would take 61,000 Chilean pesos to make $100. It appears, and rightfully so, that paper money has an extrinsic value of whatever a country decides that it has.

Some nations, in order to remedy inflationary and debt-oriented problems, arbitrarily change their money to a more appealing sounding increment. For instance, one of the proposed solutions to our current overly encumbered societal economics has been to *issue new money*, exchanging it for the old currency.

If the new money (*let's call it* **Dullards**, *for the hypothetical's sake*) was exchanged for dollars at a rate of two dollars to one Dullard that would immediately mean your $100,000 mortgage on your house would be worth 50,000 Dullards and the payments would be decreased *by half*.

Since the same ratio would be applied to our income, the actual end result would be virtually identical to where we are now. The money owed by the American government would also be reduced by half, though *the value of the debt* would remain the same.

It is actually more desirable, at least for the American government, to encourage inflation. You see, if inflation were 100% in a year that would mean the value of the dollar would have gone down by half.

It would, therefore mean, although it would still take $100 to pay off $100 in debt, the $100 used to pay of the debt would only have half the value.

So, in a *perverse sort of way*, we would be using fewer dollars and it would be getting twice as easy to pay off the debt formerly paid by a stronger dollar.

If, due to inflation, our $10 an hour salary increases as a result of 1000% inflation, in one year (and as we saw in the first chapter, it is not unusual for hyperinflation to generate inflation rates of 1000% per month), that salary would increase to $100 per hour.

At a full 40 hour work week, that would mean $17,333 per month income. If your mortgage is payable at a contractually agreed upon rate of $750 per month (including principal and interest), you can see it would not take long to pay off that mortgage.

Of course, that does not take into consideration the equally increased cost of food, gas, clothing, etc. That would eat up much, if not all of the increased income. Is the money we have owned by us?

I think we can see it truly is not. It is a tool that is under the control of whatever government that issues the money. It can be manipulated, confiscated, and even made illegal, should that government decide to do so.

If Roosevelt could issue and executive order, on April 5, 1933, to make it illegal to "hoard" (in other words "own") gold, how easy would it be for our government to make the Federal Reserve Notes illegal and start making sure you are paid in a new form of currency, which could be a new paper currency, a digital currency (something similar to bitcoins), some form of precious metals, or another arbitrary medium of exchange?

Are there ways of making sure you are protected from our own government's monetary policies and fiscal ineptitude? Please stay with me, I have an answer coming up.

## Can Protected Retirement Accounts Be in Jeopardy?

A retirement account, like a 401-K or an IRA, or a Roth IRA, are all private retirement savings accounts that have been designed to provide as much in earnings and retirement income as possible. There are a lot of varying parameters that affect the returns and thus the total amount of available funds at the time of retirement.

A good 401-K has, over the past three to five years, provided a good return on the investment through stock portfolio management or mutual funds. Some of them have even invested in REITs (Real Estate Investment Trusts) that, in turn, invest in real estate transactions and either hold properties to rent or buy and sell for substantial profits.

Although the mortgage meltdown and subsequent stock market devaluation caused the value of many 401- Ks to plummet, over the past four or five years they have, for the most part, recovered or at least regained a fair amount of their value from before the decline.

An article online, published February 1, 2014, "Retirement plan helps those with no 401(k), but not much", *by Chuck Jaffe,* outlines several problems with the myRA program as proposed by Obama.

Probably the most perplexing problem is the limitation of no more than $15,000 in the account. Anything above $15,000 has to be transferred to a Roth IRA.The minimal interest is based on the G-Fund, which in 2012 paid out 1.47%. It is more than what banks were paying on their accounts however it is still less than inflation.

So while the account balance grows, it still results in less purchasing power. Since Roth IRAs pay returns based on investments, which could be less than what a myRA might pay, the myRA goes contrary to the idea behind 401-K plans, which continue to pay with compounded interest on the total amount, regardless of how large the account is.

Since anything comprehensive would have to be approved by Congress, this myRA is designed for middle class and working class workers who don't have an employer large enough to provide 401K plans for their employees.

In an online article by Geoffrey Pike dated *Friday, February 7th, 2014* entitled: *"Will the Government Take Your 401(k)? They're Coming for your Retirement,"* He writes,
**"If there is a confiscation of 401(k) accounts, it will happen subtly. The government isn't going to announce one day that everyone has to fork over half of his or her retirement account. If they did this, they would have a revolution on their hands"**

Instead, small and subtle measures will be put into place. For example, the government might set up a guaranteed retirement fund that is backed by the full faith and credit of the U.S. government (*whatever that means*).

You would have the voluntary option —at least at first —of putting some of your 401(k) money into this special retirement account that would supposedly give you guaranteed safety and security for your money.

If the government deems this successful, then it could eventually force everyone to put a certain portion of their retirement accounts in this particular fund.

Meanwhile, the government would treat this fund like it treats the Social Security trust fund. The politicians would simply spend the money and write a bunch of worthless IOUs for the special fund.

The beginning of such a plan may have just started with Obama's new "MyRA" proposal. This program could eventually be expanded beyond just lower income people. Eventually, the politicians would try to gradually convert it from a voluntary program to a mandatory program.
It would turn into *Social Security Part 2*.

According to the Investment Company Institute (Global) article, *Retirement Assets Total $17.5 Trillion in Fourth Quarter 2010:* - *"Washington, DC, April 13, 2011 - total U.S. retirement assets were $17.5 trillion as of December 31, 2010, up 5.2 percent in the fourth quarter of 2010 and up 9.1 percent for the year. Retirement savings accounted for 37 percent of all household financial assets in the United States at year-end 2010."*

Since it is now nearly five years later, one can assume retirement savings accounts have increased, probably in line with the increase of our national debt. This is a huge amount of money, just sitting there and is an even "huger" temptation for politicians. I don't think it is a coincidence that the debt is about the same as retirement savings accounts.

We Americans have enjoyed so much presumed anonymity and prosperity over the last hundred years (even factoring in the depressions and recessions), we have come to think that our money is safe as long as it is in a government-approved retirement savings vehicle.

I think it is far more likely that the government will, at some point, not be able to resist the temptation of tapping into our "safe" retirement funds to use for their political gain although that would destroy our faith in government.

With the possibility our "benevolent" government confiscating many of our bank accounts without even being subject to criminal charges, we need to be ever more vigilant about the money we keep in the bank, for any reason.

For example, according to *VOX-Policy and Politics*:
A North Carolina business owner is fighting to recover more than $107,000 seized by the Internal Revenue Service (IRS). The IRS took the money in a civil forfeiture proceeding last year (2014).

Lyndon McLellan, owner of L&M Convenience Mart in Fairmount, N.C. had $107,702.66 seized by the IRS last summer, according to The New York Times. The 50-year-old business owner triggered the suspicion of the federal agency when he made several cash deposits of *just under $10,000*.

As Vox reports, the law states that if one deposits more than $10,000 in cash, your bank must file a form with authorities noting the transaction. It is also illegal to "structure" deposits under $10,000 to avoid the IRS red flags.

The Times points out that under the civil forfeiture law, federal authorities can seize property tied to possible crimes, even if no charges are filed. No charges have been filed against McLellan, WGHP reported.

Last October, the IRS announced it would no longer fight structuring cases unless the money was involved in a separate illegal activity, with the U.S. Department of Justice following the IRS' path in March. Still, McLellan remains without his cash. The government not only did not have the right to take his money, without charges or even true suspicion of criminal activity, but they amended their policies to reflect the lack of that right. Nevertheless, the government still retains McLellan's money as though it were theirs. Are you feeling violated, yet?

**What Other Ways Can You Prepare For Retirement?**
There are some investments that provide a reasonably secure return on your money. We cannot be sure that Social Security benefits will be around much longer. Even if it is and it remains in effect, it may not help a great deal if the dollar becomes worthless or we experience hyperinflation.

If you are getting $1,500 to $2,000 per month and groceries go up at a rate of 10% to 50% per annum, or worse—per month, your income will obviously not keep pace.

Your buying power will be dramatically reduced. If it is not destined, at some point, to be available, it will behoove you to find a means of supplementing whatever you do have and replacing the no-longer-available Social Security due to the greatly reduced buying power thereof, or the possibility of the fund being totally wiped out.

Some of the investment possibilities that will, at least for now, keep up with or exceed actual inflation are as follows:

***Income Real Estate***—there are attractive real estate investments that can still be found in some states. As long as reliable and honorable management companies exist one does not have to be too concerned about where these opportunities present themselves.

The important thing to know is, you need to make sure you do all due diligence in checking out the true condition of the property and actual income and expenses. All too often, sellers of income property misrepresent the income and expenses and nearly always the numbers are represented as "proforma" numbers.

What that means is, "if the income were what we think it should be (which we have not been able to accomplish) and the expenses were only those items we show (and not always complete or accurate), this is what the property would be worth."
*In other words a value based on proforma is imaginary.*

Make sure you get accountant certified, actual, income and expenses before you close on a deal.

Also, knowing the actual condition of a property and not just what the listing agent or owner has decided to show you (which are often the best units) is critical to knowing whether the property is a true and worthy candidate.

When inspecting the property, make the investment to have a qualified and independent Pest Control Inspector check the property out; and that means all the units. This is not just an expense, it is an insurance policy.

*First and Second Notes and Trust Deeds*—most private notes, which is what I am talking about here—bear interest rates much higher than bank savings accounts or CDs.

Private financing can bear interest at rates between 6% and 12% per annum. These notes can be for periods of between 6 months and 10 years. Sometimes they can even go longer, but I can't say I would advise a longer period of time to tie up your money.

Like income real estate, there are some rules you should never compromise on. You should make sure the amount of the trust deed (*or deeds* if more than one) does not exceed 70% of the true market value of the property securing the note.

True market value is the value indicated by an independent appraisal, which is normally paid for by the borrower. The higher the interest rate you charge, the more likely it will be defaulted on. Of course, if the value is there, foreclosing on the note might actually be beneficial.
It is, however, always a hassle. If there is a first note and trust deed ahead of you, you will be obliged to keep it current and/or pay the arrearages in order to preserve your right to foreclose ahead of the first note.

Make sure you have recorded a request for notice of default that would require the senior note holder to notify you if they are going into default.

*Similar to doing notes secured by a deed of trust, is purchasing seasoned notes;* ones that have been around for a while and have a record of being paid regularly. This strategy can be even more lucrative, because those notes that are being sold are often discounted, sometimes by as much as 50%, when the note holder is in a position where he/she needs to get cash quickly.

The same criteria apply when buying notes as when creating them. Make sure there is enough equity in the property securing the note.

***Tax Lien Certificates***—these are often overlooked as an investment vehicle. It is a little more difficult to research all the properties in a given area that are delinquent on their property taxes.

Some states just wait until the tax liens are sufficiently mature and then sell the property, others, looking to create useable funds to take care of county fiscal needs, will sell a property owner's lax lien and the owner is then responsible for paying the 13% to 24% interest on the lien when they redeem the lien and pay it back. At that point, you will receive your original investment back along with the accrued interest on the lien.

There are companies that provide all the research and lists of properties that have been selected as good candidates for purchasing those liens.

Most people are happy to get the higher interest these investments offer, but some manage to follow through to foreclosure against the property.
The equities that can be created by a tax lien being foreclosed upon can be *significant*.
Tax liens are considered superior to every other lien, including mortgages, which means any junior liens are wiped out upon foreclosing of the tax lien. Since the liens are always satisfied in some fashion, these can be very low risk investments.

The key is making sure the property on which you are purchasing the lien has adequate value to either insure repayment or sale-ability when the time to sell presents itself.

As you can see, there are a number of long and short term investments that have historically been reliable and generous return type investments, in America. There are also similar foreign investments that are equally viable, although somewhat more difficult to inspect and manage.

It would be wise to investigate every such investment that comes your way. The advantage to international investments is that you are isolated from the poorly managed dollar as it continues its downward spiral.

Your money would ideally be kept in a foreign bank and in a foreign currency. Make sure you have selected a currency that is not dependent on the dollar.

# Purchase Income Producing Assets

## Which Assets Provide Both Security and Better Than Inflation Returns?

There are so many different vehicles for investing; I will only go into a few of the more secure types of investments, here. Putting your money into a bank or bank product is not what it used to be.

In a savings account, one can count themselves lucky to get even one half of one percent interest on their money. With a CD or T-Bill, one might, and I repeat, might be able to get enough to offset inflation, but that is not even a given. If all we can do is offset inflation, we have not been able to increase the savings enough to also increase the buying power of the money in the account.

Investing in the stock market can be lucrative, if one knows what they are doing and manages to pick the right stocks, provide insurance with "put options" or make sure there is a good trailing "stop-loss". Mutual funds are managed by various companies and some of them are good.
That means they might actually be able to increase your investment beyond what inflation eats up.

Having said that, it is also possible to lose your shirt in the stock market and in mutual funds, which is just another way of investing in the stock market.
Although most people don't actually consider gold and silver to be investments, they are certainly an insurance policy against total loss.

Where the value of a stock can go to zero, gold and silver will always retain a value of some amount. Mutual funds are generally a basket of stocks and securities, which provides some insurance in the sense that if one stock goes down; it is unlikely that all the stocks will go down at the same time.

If, however, there is a decline in most of the stocks, as happened when the Twin Towers were hit, then mutual funds are likely to, and historically have gone down, too.

Real estate has, over the years, been an investment that has been pretty secure and will, over time, provide a return that one would expect to outpace inflation. I have been a real estate broker for nearly 35 years and can say that I have seen real estate pretty much hold its own during that time.

Of course, there are times, like the mortgage melt down in the late 2000s, which, by the way, was engineered by both the dictates of our own government and compliance by banks and lenders that the value of real estate can go down, sometimes significantly.

There were many people who lost an incredible amount of money due to foreclosures on mortgages that were onerous and/or usurious. There were also many who lost value on homes or real estate they wanted to sell, simply because there was a lack of investors in the declining market, along with buyers disappearing as a result of homeowners not being able to sell their homes and buy "up".

These who normally would be buyers in a real estate market ended up as renters or even having to move into homes with their families. Here it is seven or so years later and most markets have not only recovered, but even exceeded the values they enjoyed before the mortgage/real estate bubble burst.

One could argue that, if investors had invested wisely in real estate and not taken advantage of sub-prime loans, they would now be in a better financial position than when they originally purchased their real estate.

Reports from San Francisco, just recently on the news, show that the average "small" single family residence has a value between one million and two million dollars.

That has been spurred by a combination of extremely low interest rates (purchase loans bearing between 2.9% and 3.9% on ten and thirty year loans) and lack of supply.

People are just not putting their homes on the market out of fear they will not be able to replace it with something equivalent for the money they realize from the sale of their home.

San Francisco is not the only city where that is the case. New home starts have, once again, become a statistically relevant factor in market sales.

Over the past seven years many people who had pulled their money out of the stock market and were sitting on their savings, were buying homes as rentals and in areas that were not intended for the rental market when built.

The normal standard of needing the monthly rent to be at least one percent of the purchase price went out the door once people realized that if they paid cash and could get an annualized return (after taxes, insurance, and maintenance) of between 4% and 5%, there was no reason to leave it in a bank at less than one percent.

The cash buyers were so prolific, for several of those years, that it actually started driving up the values, again. People who just wanted to purchase a home to live in were generally hampered by needing to qualify for financing and not being able to come up with an adequate down-payment to keep their monthly payments down. Sellers were and
are generally far more interested in selling to someone who can pay cash and close quickly, even if they have to discount it a bit to get cash.

That trend has lessened, but there are still large REITs that have been set up for the express purpose of purchasing blocks of foreclosed homes at huge discounts.

Banks have had to drop the prices of millions of homes and bundle them in packages of twenty, thirty and more, homes to get them off their ledgers.

Today, the primary detriment to the real estate market is the continued loss of jobs and reduction of wages in the potential buyers. Obamacare, (the Affordable Care Act) or more accurately *Obamadon'tcare*, has created an environment where employers are electing to employ people for less than full time so they don't have to provide the costly health insurance under the (un) Affordable Health Care Act.

In fact, as part-time employees, the employers are often able to pay a lower hourly wage, which only exacerbates the problem.

**Is Real Estate Safe?**
There is a saying, "God doesn't make any more real estate." I suppose one could argue that alluvium, which is formed by eroding soil from a higher plane to a lower one, could be the creation of new ground for development, but that is a stretch since it generally doesn't involve a great deal of area.

The same is true for deposition of magma (lava) that increases the perimeter of an island, for instance. Unfortunately, it takes a long time for that "new" land to become useable. It also bears the risk of being in the path of the next lava flow. That would not be an attractive characteristic for development.

The factors we covered earlier, make a strong argument for investing in real estate. Purchasing a home is still one of the most expensive purchases a family makes during their lifetime. I would argue that, even though the purchase is more utilitarian for the consumer, it is still an investment. If one purchases with the right criteria, meaning they make sure they don't finance more than 80% of the home's value, and insure that the principal, interest, taxes, and insurance (PITI), don't exceed about 40% of their income, the purchase should work for them.

Assuming they are able to remain employed in a job that continues their income at or above the level they received at the time of the purchase, they can enjoy long-term appreciation, even when the market occasionally declines for short periods of time.
The same holds true for investors who purchase homes to hold and rent.

The amount one pays for a home should, ideally, not exceed a rent to cost ratio of 1%. Most of the time, that 1% should be sufficient to pay Principal, Interest, Taxes, and Insurance (PITI) and maintenance and still end up with a positive net income at the end of the year.

Many people looking for good investments shy away from an investment where they think they will have to visit the property in the middle of the night to unplug toilets. That is unfortunate, because there are still good property management companies that will take care of the work for you and make sure the cost is held to a minimum.

There are also real estate investments where one does not have to deal with toilets. For instance a mini-storage property provides income and almost no maintenance and certainly doesn't have problems with toilets. Bare land that can be rented out for livestock or to create producing farms can also be a nearly trouble-free investment.

Whatever you invest in, if it is real estate, just make sure it has all the right numbers and do your "due diligence" before buying. Make sure you don't pay too much and that the property is not a toxic or environmental waste zone and that the condition of a house will not require a small fortune to repair and maintain.

Do all your inspections to ascertain the true condition of the property. If you do all these things, then, indeed, real estate is a safe and lucrative investment.

## Do Assets Need To Be in America Or Should You Consider International?

The one thing we need to consider, in America today, is that our money may soon no longer be the reserve currency.

There are certain benefits that go along with our country having the reserve currency, from stronger and more in-demand currency to being able to print more without the approval of other countries. Germany, for instance, cannot print more euros without approval of the rest of the European Union.

Chile can print more of their pesos (which today is at 611 pesos per US dollar) without permission from other countries, but that would quickly devalue their money on the currency exchange market. That is true of any currency that is not a reserve currency.

We, in America, seem to ignore the fact that, even as the reserve currency, there is a limit as to what other countries will accept. The arrogance America shows in wantonly diluting the value of individual dollars by printing so many of them is more than foolish.

If we purchase U.S. assets it should be pretty clear the devaluation of the dollar will eventually affect the credibility and value of those assets. If
you own a rental and the declining value of the dollar spurs an injurious inflation rate, let's say for instance, a rate of 100% per year, there is no certainty a tenant who would have to earn twice what he or she did at the beginning of the year, would have to pay more rent, unless there is an inflation clause in the rental agreement that says the tenant's rent will increase in line with inflation.

If there is no such clause in the rental agreement, that means you as the landlord would still be getting the same amount of dollars, each month, but they would only go half as far in purchasing power.

Investments in bonds, CDs, T-Bills, etc., will continue to produce interest rates based on the dollar, without regard to the decline in value of the dollar.

Any reduction of purchasing power for the dollar will result in the same reduction in the value of the dollars earned in spite of the interest earned.
It is because of such a situation that we need to at least consider investing in another country and in another currency.

Real estate in another country is not even reportable to the IRS unless it is providing an income. If you are merely accruing appreciation on the value of the property, especially if the economy in that country is good, then you are not showing a realized income and will not be taxed on it.

Since you would be receiving any income from that foreign investment in the currency of that country (as converting it to dollars would subject it to a potential spiraling downward value of the dollar) you could keep it in that currency and reap the continued stability and strength of that currency, thereby offsetting the instability of the American dollar.
Income in any currency in any country will result in taxes being owed on that income.

There are, however, certain exceptions and it would be good to research those and make sure you do not pay taxes that are not required.

It is difficult to find a foreign bank that will still accept American customers, due to the FATCA and FBAR regulations the American Congress and IRS have foisted on the world's banks, but it is still possible. The Caye Bank, in Belize, is one of those banks that still accept American customers.

Be aware those banks that do accept us are complying completely with the IRS reporting requirements. There is no legal way to avoid reporting the amount of money you have in any bank, foreign or domestic.

Having money in a foreign bank, whether in dollars or another currency, does not yet mean you will have to pay taxes on that money, unless it is income in the year of reporting that has not yet been taxed in America. It does not matter where the money is earned, the United States reserves the right to collect income taxes on that amount.

Again, there are exceptions to the rule, but they change all the time, so you need to make sure you know what the rules are in that year. There are currently ways to legally not pay income tax on up to nearly $100,000 per person or $200,000 per couple if you are living outside the US and receiving an income. Research that well, though.

You do not want to get caught abusing the rules, because the penalties can be huge.
In light of the above, I would say it is certainly an option to purchase income property in another country. Since the income generated by that property would be in the currency of that country, it would provide a hedge against the devaluation of the dollar.

For example if your euros are worth $1.08 right now and the dollar declines by 50% in the next year that would mean your euros would be worth $2.16. That would be an effective hedge. By the way, I am not suggesting you keep your money in euros. That currency is not effectively any different than the dollar in its strength in the international money market.

There is even a potential it could decline in value faster than the dollar. Just be wise and do your research when deciding what currency to keep and in which bank you keep it.

The same rules apply to securities purchased in other countries and stock markets. The important thing is to find a market in a country with a strong or strengthening currency and banking rules that allow for Americans to open accounts in their currency.

**What About the Stock Market.**
Unless you have been holed up in a cave for the last several years, you could not have helped noticing the stock market has been going up…and up…*and up!*

Although the volume of trades in the stock market has consistently been very low, the apparent optimism of the stock buyers has been very Pollyanna-like. Of course this was encouraged in large part by the Federal Reserve creating new fiat money to purchase the bonds issued in the market.

It was not real money, but investors feel that as long as there is a buyer out there, even for the bad debt of the U.S., then investing in the market must be safe. We are at an all-time high, on the DOW, of over 18,000, but that very fact means that a lot of investors see this as a reason to get into the market before it goes up even higher.

It seems crazy, but people never learn. One does not invest in the market when it is at an all-time high. Still, there is a lot of money to be made in the stock market. One can either play volatile stocks, buying
and selling at the right times (which usually requires a crystal ball), or one can invest in large, historically sound, companies that have weathered other financial crises, and that have a consistent policy of paying dividends one or more times per year. I have dabbled in the stock market and have done well at times, but have also done poorly at other times. I have come to the conclusion that there are money managers who are sound and cautious and who can make you money.

I do not feel competent to recommend any, nor do I feel like I have the wisdom to pick stocks or the points of entry into stock trades.

If you feel inclined to invest in the stock market, keep in mind when the market feels like the Feds are betraying it, for example not purchasing any more U.S. debt or raising interest rates, etc., they will abandon ship so fast it will be hard to recognize the jump ship order in a timely fashion or even to keep up with those jumpers.

# Make Efforts to Get Free & Clear
# With All Your Assets

### Why Get Out Of Debt?
Debt is today's number one social and economic cancer. The *18 trillion dollar debt* of our government is symptomatic and also causal when it comes to devaluing the dollar and reducing the credibility of the US government. It is no less important and harmful for each of us in this country than our own debt.

Our economic societal policies not only make it easy to incur debt, but is often implicit it pushing individuals into entering into debt even when one is otherwise reluctant to do so.

Credit cards, for instance, are often required to use as a form of identification. Staying in hotels or motels often require a credit card to be swiped, even when one intends to pay cash.

There are so many instances where one is required to agree to credit, even when that is not the intent, and those instances often are resolved by making a spur of the moment decision to go ahead and put the charges on the card. It often seems, at the moment, to be the easier path to follow.

The more debt you incur, the worse your credit rating. It is often too easy to just give in to the temptation put the charges on your card.
Oddly, the more you are in debt, the easier it seems to be to get more credit, whether it is a new card, financing a purchase, or obligating one's self to more products on credit.

If you feel a need to keep credit cards, it is wise to make sure you pay off any outstanding balance at the end of each billing cycle. Not only will you normally avoid interest charges, but you will enjoy the freedom you feel by not having the debt.

As mentioned above, credit is a form of economic cancer. It is something you may not and, in fact, probably don't want, but it breeds and multiplies in your pocket book. Not only do charges somehow get incurred even when you don't necessarily want them, but the debt continues to grow as a result of the interest charges.

It is in everyone's best interest to try to eradicate both the ease and temptation to charge, and to reduce the amount of debt to zero, as soon as is feasible.

Debt is the same as servitude. Until that debt is paid off, you are a servant to the creditor. Think about your mortgage (which by the way you are paying even if you only think you are paying rent. The landlord is using your rent to pay mortgage, taxes, insurance, and maintenance).

Even with a nominal interest rate on a mortgage it is not uncommon to pay several hundred thousand dollars of interest over the life of the loan.
You are not actually putting your money to effective use. Interest is good for the lender, but not good for you.

Should you pay off or try to get rid of debt? I actually can't think of a single instance where it is good to perpetuate payment on debt. I have heard it argued that today's low interest rates makes borrowed money so cheap, we can't afford to not borrow the money.

If you could borrow the money at 4% interest and put it into a guaranteed investment that will return 10%-12%, perhaps that would be a good argument.

Unfortunately, that form of what amounts to arbitrage only seems to present itself in the best of economies. Since those economies don't seem to last, it is a move one would have to take after a great deal of consideration.

## How to Get Out Of Debt.

Perhaps it is somewhat presumptuous for me to suggest I know how to direct you to get out of debt.

There are, however, certain immutable ways to deal with ridding one's self of debt. None of them are easy, but our long term predisposition to take on debt is something that takes a while to overcome and rectify.

The first and foremost step toward0 getting out of debt is to stop charging things and buying on credit. It is fundamentally counter-productive to attempt to pay of your debt while continuing to charge things. I know in a day and age where many people buy much of what they need online, it is so easy to pay for those purchases with a credit card.

I have found it possible to order items on the Internet and send in a check or a money order to pay where, upon receipt of the funds, they ship you your product. It is not as fast as paying with a credit card, but at least it does not increase your debt.

One of the best ways I have heard to reduce your outstanding debt, especially if you have several credit cards that are all at or near their limit, is to select one of those credit cards, usually the one with the lowest debt, and resolve to pay more than the minimum, each month.

You will have to determine for yourself how much more you can pay from the income you have each month. Obviously, the more you can pay the better. If you can afford an extra $50, per month, make sure you pay that extra amount every month.

You might be surprised at just how quickly that card will be paid off. Once it is paid off, you will apply the minimum payment that was due each month on that card and combine it with the extra $50 you were paying and pay that amount toward the debt on another card.

So now, perhaps your payment toward the next card will be $75 more than the minimum amount. Repeat the process on each succeeding card. Each time you do this, the amount being applied toward a remaining card will be even greater. Each succeeding card will end up getting paid off faster than the previous.
There are numerous debt counselors who specialize in helping you get out of debt.

Usually it requires them contacting the creditors and working out a payment plan that works toward getting you out of debt in the shortest time possible.

Needless to say, there are a lot of different ways of reducing and eliminating debt, but the most sound processes require limiting or eliminating the perpetuation of debt by not charging items and not purchasing things on credit.

This requires resolve and is particularly difficult because our own government is in debt way over its eyeballs and shows no inclination to curb that spending spree.

They do not seem to get the message, "Our kids and grandkids are going into debt to finance your political aspirations." It is, for your financial security and future fiscal wellbeing, so important to eliminate your debt.

This would include your residence. Imagine, by having increased your monthly payment on your house, suddenly being debt free and have your mortgage paid off. All of a sudden, you are no longer in a position to serve the lender.

Your total monthly obligations will drop off enormously. You have now put yourself into a position of being able to save your money (although I am not a big proponent of banks) to pay cash for anything from toys to cars.

It literally can put you in the driver's seat where you are in charge. Don't take this lightly. It might be one of the most important things you can do in your adult life.

**A Penny Saved Is A Penny Earned.**
I have watched family and friends spending money on things that have no real value in life or even to their level of comfort. Much of the time, those expenditures are for things that are for fun and games, or things they didn't know they "needed" until they saw them.

I know grown men who spend a great deal of time playing video games, which they have to buy and which they have to spend time on that could otherwise be spent being constructive or profitable. I agree that everyone has a different standard of what is important in their life.

One needs to realize, however, that time and money spent on things that do not edify or benefit the family and one's security in the long run, is time you will never be able to recapture.

My wife and I often joke about bending over to pick up pennies. We both do not hesitate to pick up even the pennies we see on the ground.

Many people think pennies are so worthless it makes no sense to waste the time and effort to pick them up. I can't count the times I have been in a store and was just a penny short, in change, and had to break a one dollar bill or larger. That happens less when I take the time to pick up pennies off the sidewalk or street.
Since 1982, the penny has only 2.5% copper (plated only) and 97.5% zinc. Copper had grown so valuable in the industrial market and electronics, pennies had as much as $.03 worth of copper each.

There are two ways of accumulating money. The first is to spend time wisely generating money as income. The second, and perhaps more important, is to make sure you can keep as much of what you generate as possible.

That means wise spending and doing without those things that do not and never will benefit your long term retention and availability of money. We have already discussed some of the investments you can put your money into that will not only aid you now and provide for a hedge against inflation, but provide a long term capital gain and lower taxation on that gain.

I can't say I do not want to have toys and do fun things. In fact, my wife and I love to travel and spend a fair amount of time doing so. That is not without cost and means there are other things we feel we cannot or at least will not do, in order to save some of our net income for investing in things that will accrue to our future betterment. Frugality can be carried to an extreme.

One should not overlook putting money into things that provide knowledge and tap into other learned people's recommendations and advice. There is no one who recognizes this more than my wife, Evelyn.

She is tireless when it comes to taking care of me and the household, but she is equally tireless when it comes to increasing her knowledge and awareness in how to better ourselves financially.

While there are some costs to gaining that knowledge, she recognizes the value of what she can learn from experts. Some of her favorites are people like Porter Stansberry at Stansberry and Associates, Dr. Steve Sjuggerud of Steve Sjuggerud's Daily Wealth, Doug Casey – International Man, Simon Black – Sovereign Man, and James Rickard, author of "The Death of Money: The Coming Collapse of the International Monetary System." There is a cost to acquiring their advice, whether it is through signing up for their various newsletters, their confidential reports, or purchasing their books, but what you will learn from these kinds of men or women is more than you will get from four years of college at a small fraction of the cost.

## Can We Trust Financial Consultants?

In the last section, I made reference to a number of experts in the economy. They make recommendations on how to prepare for the coming financial meltdown.

Most of these people are financial consultants of some degree. There are many more that I have not mentioned. Simply calling oneself a financial consultant does not make them one, nor does it in any fashion make them a good one.

I have some friends my age and others much older who have managed to put their money into the hands of financial consultants who have kept their clients well ahead of the markets and kept them comfortable. That does not mean they did not experience a real, tangible, loss, during the 2008 and onward recession.

They have, however managed to help them recover and even exceed their previous returns on investments. I do not know the financial consultants personally, but I know there are some very good ones out there.

When I talk to the parties I was referring to, though, there is a total lack of awareness of the potential of a real financial crisis in our country and even in the world. They not only don't know about this potential, but in their current comfort with how things are going, they refuse to believe anything can happen to a country that has not only provided them a comfortable retirement and life, but has even recovered from the recession most realize was as bad or worse than the Great Depression.

How can such prosperity and worry-free-living point to such a destructive and financially devastating end? How, Indeed! Never having gone personally through the types of things that have besieged other countries (see Chapter I), one can easily say, "That can't happen here. This is the United States." There were those who were astute enough to recognize what was coming in each of the past financial crises.

They put themselves on a journey of finding not only a place where they could be shielded from what was to come, but found a way to take much, if not all, their worldly goods and fortune with them.

Good financial consultants may be great at helping you stay ahead of inflation, preventing unnecessary losses, and providing you a comfortable return on your investments to supplement or even replace your salary or social security.

The biggest concern I have about such consultants is their self interest in their ability to make money by providing these outlined services. If they were to counsel you to get your money out of the country and into another, safer, currency and then for you to find a way to have a place of residence outside the country; perhaps even acquire a different passport (which, by the way, can sometimes be as easy as applying for one in a country from which your immediate ancestors came), they would, in effect, be cutting their noses off to spite their faces. If you were to do all these things, they would be losing a client.

It would be kind of like a doctor who has discovered a cure for cancer that costs a minimal amount of money, but upon administration of that cure, he loses the opportunity to earn large amounts of money by administering drugs and chemotherapy. That is not likely to happen, even if there is such a cure.

Yes, I would recommend getting references to find a good financial consultant. However, whatever you do, do not hide from the inevitable. The financial meltdown and the "Death of Money" is coming.

America has experienced a banking and money crisis about every 40 years for the last 150 years. The next one will likely include the international money market and will, because of that, be far more severe. Take the necessary steps to either become a professional, with regard to your own financial situation, or at least take advantage of the experts out there who are willing, for a small tuition, to sell you their combined knowledge and expertise.

# What Happens When the Dollar
# Loses Its Value?
# (It's Already Nearly At Zero)

**What Is the Value Of A Dollar?**
We have already, in previous chapters, discussed the history of the dollar, in America. What happens to citizens, though, when one can no longer purchase anything with the dollar?

In *"What Will Happen To You When The Dollar Collapses?"* written by *Tyler Durden* at **www.zerohedge.com,** Tyler goes into some detail about what we might expect.

Rather than to present my own ideas and positions I will quote from some of the salient points of his thesis. What if our nation's currency does collapse?
"Historically, when a nation's debt exceeds its ability to repay even the interest, it can be assumed that the currency will collapse.

Typically, governments exacerbate the situation by printing large amounts of currency notes in an effort to inflate the problem away, or at least postpone it."

*"The greater the level of debt, the more dramatic the inflation must* **be to counter it.** *The more dramatic the inflation, the greater the danger that hyperinflation will take place.*

*No government has ever been able to control hyperinflation. If it occurs, it does so quickly and always ends with a crash."*

"Although there are observers (myself included) who frequently discuss what a reserve-currency crash would mean to the world, there is little or no discussion as to how this would impact people on the street level, and perhaps that discussion should begin."

Truly, this is where the rubber meets the road. You and I are the people on the street level. If hyperinflation hits and we can no

longer go to the grocery store and purchase a half gallon of milk for $3.00, but instead have to spend $40 or $50 for that same gallon one week and $100 to
$150 the next week, we are no longer going to be able to afford to buy groceries; at least not with the income we currently have.

The author goes on to say, "When currencies crash, the state often **tries to float a new currency.** Sometimes, it's accepted, sometimes not. Generally, the people of the country (and those trading within the country) move immediately to 'the next best thing'.

In 2009, when the Zimbabwe dollar crashed, several currencies were used, but the US dollar was the clear favorite, as it was the world's reserve currency and therefore the most 'spendable' currency."

"Not surprisingly, the Zimbabwean government fought the use of the dollar, as they wanted to retain control of the economy and the people.
People were therefore penalized (sic) for using the US dollar and other currencies."
Can you think of a currency the American population could turn to if the dollar loses its value? There is currently no other form of money in the world that Americans would feel comfortable with. The euro is no better off than the dollar and will probably meet its demise before the dollar.

Europeans are generally comfortable enough to consider using the dollar when their currency declines, but in all likelihood the dollar will follow suit in short order. That is why the author goes on to say, "The big question that is generally not being discussed is: The day after the crash (and thereafter), what will be the currency that is used to buy a bag of groceries, a tank of petrol, a meal at a restaurant?

Certainly, the *need* will be immediate and will be on a national level in each impacted country, affecting everyone."

Tyler Durden points out three things that will happen if America creates an equally valueless form of digital currency.
1. It will allow the US government to blame paper currencies for the crash, in order to distract the public from recognizing (sic) that the government itself is the culprit.
2. It will allow the US government to create a currency system that disallows the holding of tradable currency by the population—that is, a debit card would be created by banks through which *all* transactions must pass, assuring that *all* transactions are processed by (and thereby subject to the control of) a bank.
3. It will allow the US government to have knowledge of every penny earned and spent by any individual or organization, allowing for direct-debit income taxation.

Any attempt on the part of the citizenry to use any other form of currency, including precious metals, to purchase goods and services will in all likelihood be declared to be illegal, which means much of our economy will go underground. Certainly precious metals, and especially silver rounds, will become an obvious choice of currency.

The problem is, most people do not have any silver or gold. Although governments (except perhaps the USA) are stockpiling gold and silver, people in the
USA don't seem to be getting the message.

Most people think of gold and silver as an investment, when in reality they are merely insurance policies against loss in the event (and I believe certainty) of the crash of the US dollar.

Since the value of any paper currency is in the presumed backing the government provides for the currency, its real value is zero. Paper money = fiat currency = no true and intrinsic value.

It would obviously be better to have stocked away something of real value that one can readily use for goods and services (especially groceries and gasoline) when the time comes.

Some suggest large quantities of the most popular ammunition (which is already experiencing restrictions in some areas), or large quantities of batteries of the most popular sizes, or obviously gold and silver. There are other forms of trading currency and they are only limited by our own imaginations.

**Fiat Currency**
Paper money (fiat currency) is money that is created out of thin air. I know I have been redundant about this, but it is crucial that you understand this principal.

If I give you a piece of paper on which I have written "IOU twenty (20) ounces of silver or the equal value in goods and/or services" in return for a certain number of hours you have worked for me, and assure you I will honor that note (IOU) at any time, that would be the equivalent to receiving a certain number of dollar bills for the same amount of work.

If I die or my supply of goods and resources for services go away, suddenly the note I gave you is worthless. The same is true when the government is no longer able to stand behind its currency, because the cost of backing the money is more than what the money is worth. Suddenly, our dollars have no more value.
The country is then faced with a need to have a currency everyone will recognize. If it is the same government issuing a new fiat currency, they will still be faced with a lack of faith by the people in the new currency.

That is why people will turn to something with intrinsic value. The only things that have intrinsic value and are small enough to store and carry are things like gold, silver, and diamonds/jewels and, as mentioned above, things others will value.

Gold and silver that are minted and stamped .999 pure and made by governments of the world and have been readily accepted as reliably pure sources, will be a lot more discernable as items of specific value than would jewels. There is no easy way for a layman to determine the purity and value of diamonds, rubies, etc.

Once again, remember that paper money—in and of itself—has no intrinsic value, it is only at the whim of the bearer of that paper currency, or the recipient, that it has any value. Don't get caught with a
wheel barrow full of $100 bills (as they did in the Weimar Regime with
German marks) that is still not enough to pay for those groceries. Buy
gold and silver, now, while it is still legal and available. An ounce of
silver right now is only about $16 to $18 dollars. Try to buy several
each month and save them for a time when you can't buy anything with
our paper money.

**The Full Faith and Credit Of the United States Government.**
For many years, in the history of our nation, people could rely on a very secure investment vehicle called United States Savings Bonds.
Although the interest rates were not enormous (usually only between 3- 5%) it was a certainty that the redemption value would be there. It was backed by the full faith and credit of the United States Government.

Today, while the US government goes out of its way to honor debt to other countries, it is becoming a very risky bet on the value of money it owes to its own people.

Our government takes money out of the social security trust fund to spend on frivolous benefits and expenditures that are not voted on by the American people. The insolvent position of our government causes it to take money from us, in the form of taxes, fines, fees, and confiscations, to try to make up for their self-inflicted shortfalls.

There is, in fact, no credibility for the US government. Our world standing has declined so far that even governments like Germany and France are trying to get the US government to return their gold, ostensibly in Fort Knox, to them.

The US Government is not even willing to let them "see" the gold held in their name. Could it be that this gold is no longer there? Could it be we have either sold off or rented out that gold to create some short-lived currency or benefit for ourselves?

I believe this is actually the case. Instead of letting the German officials lay eyes on the gold we are supposedly holding for them, the US government has agreed to pay it back to them in seven years. Why would we do that if we still had the gold? It is obviously (assuming the gold is sitting in those vaults) not earning us anything.

If it is there, we are not allowed to use it. The only explanation is, we don't have it any more and it will take us a while to get it back in order to return it to them. So much for the "Full Faith And Credit Of The United States Government."

Is it any wonder our credibility on the world stage is declining? Is it any wonder the Chinese Government is establishing the Asian Infrastructure Investment Bank (AIIB) to replace the International Funds Bank?

Is it any wonder there have been over forty of our allies who, against the recommendation of Obama and his administration, have signed onto the charter of the bank?
All signs point to there being no more "faith and credit" in our government.
This is a one billion mark bill from around 1924

# Are Foreign Currencies
# the Answer?

**What Do We See the Currencies Of Other Countries Doing?**
In the last few months, we have watched the dollar increase in value against other currencies. Although the dollar is weak and getting weaker, other major currencies have suffered even greater weakness.

The euro, Swiss frank, British pound, etc., have been declining in value faster than the dollar. That gives the impression that the dollar is gaining in value. Quite the opposite is true. The dollar has a couple of advantages.

Since it is still the generally accepted reserve currency for the world (a standing that will soon be no more), it is still seen as the currency in which all debts need to be resolved.

Since we still can and do print more money and use this "monopoly money" to pay our debts, the world still seems to value it more than other currencies.

Now, recently, we have been watching the euro, Swiss franc, and British pound, increase in value against the dollar. In fact, with the decline in oil prices and our inability to store more oil or sell oil to other countries, there has been a real decline in the value of the dollar.

This game of increasing and decreasing values of one currency against another will continue for some time, with no real goal posts to try to achieve on any side.

There is actually an exchange called the Forex, on which currencies are bought and sold just like stocks on the stock exchange. Some people make fortunes or lose fortunes buying and selling currencies. It is a volatile commodity and difficult to predict, so one needs to use discretion in determining which currencies to buy and sell at which times.

There is, however, a lot of talk, in the financial field, recommending opening an account in a foreign bank and in a different currency than the dollar. There are currencies that are strong and which are increasing consistently in value against the euro and dollar. It would be worthwhile to take some time to research the historical trend of currencies to determine which one might be the best to invest in.

Financial consultants, mentioned earlier in this book, actually research and recommend currencies that have the potential to strengthen or stay strong against the US dollar. The point is, holding on to the dollar could be very destructive and would provide no security as the dollar declines in value.

**The United States Dollar Is the Main Reserve Currency. Do We Really Have To Worry?**
The United States Dollar has had a long history of being strong, well-managed, and acknowledged everywhere in the world as a medium of exchange.
It has been so well accepted as the currency that is most widely accepted, that no one, in general, had been questioning that status.

In fact, it has been so unquestioned that politicians, beginning with the President, feel they can bully the world's banks into complying with whatever America says they should do. Recently, the United States government fined a foreign bank billions of dollars to show them they should not be doing what America does not want them to do.

On July 1, 2014, Business Insider published an article by Steve Slater and Michelle Price called, *"The Huge US Fines On Foreign Banks Are Having The Intended Effect"*. It says, "Financiers may grumble that the United States is acting like an imperial power in punishing foreign banks for dealings far beyond U.S. territory, but in the end they are more likely to bow to Washington than kick against its dollar muscle.

Last week, French politicians and business leaders demanded an end to the global dominance of the U.S.

currency - and hence of the U.S. banking system - after a New York court fined French bank BNP Paribas $9 billion for doing business in Sudan, Iran and Cuba."
France is not alone and now there is a strong movement on the part of the Asian Infrastructure Investment Bank to help the Chinese yuan take over the role of being the reserve currency.

The fact so many of our allies have readily and speedily signed on to the AIIB shows the concerted efforts on the part of many other countries to get rid of the bullying tyranny they have had to deal with for so long.

So you see, even with the benefits of being the main reserve currency, which have certainly allowed America to get away with a lot of actions other countries have not been able to allow themselves without the normal accompanying consequences, the dollar is on a clear path to lose its role as the reserve currency.

Stansberry and Associate' researcher, Sjuggerud, suggests it could happen in October 2015. When and if that happens, all those delayed consequences will descend on the American people. Although the dollar will still be one of the several reserve currencies, if Sjuggerud is correct, it will no longer be the dominant one.

It is not completely clear just what consequences will happen and when, but it is clear the American politicians are totally in the dark about what is coming. In fact, the arrogance they display is nothing short of incredible. It is we, the American People, who will have to suffer and pay for their indiscretions.

If you are reading this after October of 2015, you will probably have already seen some of the consequences.

Having the status of reserve currency will obviously not protect us from what is coming. It will be up to us to provide our own security against what is to come.

**The Petro Dollar and Its Downside.**
When trying to define just what is meant by Petro dollar, Wikipedia writes, "In an effort to prop up the value of the dollar, Richard Nixon negotiated a deal with Saudi Arabia that in exchange for arms and protection they would denominate all future oil sales in U.S. dollars.

Subsequently, the other OPEC countries agreed to similar deals, thus ensuring a global demand for U.S. dollars and allowing the U.S. to export some of its inflation.

Since these dollars did not circulate within the country and thus were not part of the normal money supply, economists felt another term was necessary to describe the dollars received by petroleum exporting countries (OPEC) in exchange for oil.

So the term petrodollar was coined by Georgetown University economics professor, Ibrahim Oweiss.
Once, again, it is a case of the American Government insinuating itself into the world economy in such a way as to assure the power of the dollar and insure a revenue from every transaction of oil in OPEC nations, regardless of who was purchasing that oil.

One can argue, all day long, that it was beneficial for all Americans to have the government supported by transactions that did not result in a tax on our own citizens. The problem once again, is the resentment of the other nations of the world who were forced by the deal with the OPEC nations to purchase dollars with which to purchase oil.

America benefited from both the purchase of the dollars and from the purchase of the Saudi riyal with the dollars they had received for the purchase.

Ultimately, though, it costs the nation's purchasing the oil that much more to purchase. Don't imagine there is no resentment for that additional cost.

The U.S. is the economically supreme nation in that its dollar is the world's reserve currency. This allows it to maintain an unequaled military empire basically for free by creating worthless paper (fiat) money and/or its electronic equivalent.

Russia and China can't afford do that, because it would cause their currencies, and thus their economies, to collapse if they did. China and Russia have been instrumental in starting the trend of trade agreements that agree to use the currencies of the countries trading with one another.
Because of such agreements, there are more and more countries and thus more and more trades that are taking place without the use of the dollar.

One of the reasons the Federal Reserve has been able to get away with flooding the financial system with U.S. dollars in recent years is because the rest of the world has been soaking a lot of those dollars up. The rest of the world has needed giant piles of dollars to trade with, but what is going to happen when they don't need dollars anymore?

It is pretty clear, once the dollar is no longer in such demand and is not needed any more, that inflation will skyrocket in our economy. To this day, the power of the U.S. dollar has been one the few things holding up our economy. Once the demand for the dollar is eliminated, we are all going to be in big trouble.

# Is Bitcoin the Answer?

**Digital Currency (The Bitcoin) Is New, But Is It Safe?**
CNN- Money says, *"Bitcoin is a new currency that was created in 2009 by an unknown person using the alias Satoshi Nakamoto. Transactions are made with no middle men – meaning, no banks!*

*There are no transaction fees and no need to give your real name. More merchants are beginning to accept them: You can buy webhosting services, pizza or even manicures."*

The bitcoin is a remarkable piece of "crypto-currency" that has no physical presence and is stored in a large bank of computers that are compensated, in bitcoin, for creating the whole of the network in which the bitcoin exists.

Just like the Internet, if a large segment of the computers used for this purpose were to be deactivated, it would have little effect on the whole. There is a key that is your own private key, which cannot be duplicated or replaced. This key is required to do any transaction with bitcoins. If I purchase something with a bitcoin, I use this secret encrypted key to send a message to the web of computers authorizing the transaction and passing the coin to another.

The software that operates this digital world or economy verifies the authorization comes from me (simultaneously verifying that I am me) and that I am the true owner of the coin. It then registers the ownership of that coin in the name of the person I am transferring it to.

Of course, bitcoins remain alive and well in the digital world as long as people participating in this digital world believe in it and act on the strength of their belief; not a great deal different from paper currency.

Assuming these conditions, a bitcoin is as good as any paper money; perhaps better because the governments and banks have no control over it.

The bottom line is, Bitcoin is a means of trade that was developed which by-passes government and banking controls and manipulations.

It can be as secure as any other fiat form of currency and may be more secure in that it is harder to redirect (steal) bitcoins from the encrypted accounts.

Primarily, the only access to the bitcoin is with the secret key one gets for that purpose. If you lose, misplace, or have that secret key stolen, there is no way of replacing it or recovering it. It has increased so much in value, over the last couple years, that one bitcoin has nearly the value of one ounce of gold.

Although there are businesses and investors who do accept the bitcoin, one cannot say, at this point, just how universal that acceptance will become.

It is possible to create a bitcoin account and maintain it anonymously and without government knowledge or oversight. That may provide some relief, albeit illegal relief, from taxation.

The government cannot tax something they don't know exists. That, however, is the reason one must assume the government will find a way to track, monitor, and tax these transactions. Right now it is viewed as income and sales tax evasion.

To show you how intent the US government is on controlling digital currency, the US Financial Crimes Enforcement Network (FinCEN), have just issued the first-ever 'civil enforcement action' against a virtual currency.

You see, Ripple Labs created a native virtual currency called 'XRP', which is the second largest in the world after bitcoin, when measured by market capitalization. Although Ripple Labs has done nothing to break the law, the government sees a need to start intimidation tactics to subdue actions that are perfectly legal under current law.

As usual, be careful. It is not currently illegal to have and deal in bitcoins. Once the government devises ways to tax and control it, many of the current advantages will become either illegal or non-existent.

**What Are the Gurus and Pundits Saying?**
There are several things people in the know about bitcoin are saying, regarding this new form of currency.

*1. Bitcoin can help ordinary people.*
Ordinary people in Argentina are using "old Android phones" to acquire and exchange Bitcoins at a time when the government is clamping down on the trade in U.S. dollars. More remarkably, is that many of the people using bitcoin don't know much about technology — but they do know, through firsthand experience, about currencies and can recognize alternate sources of money.

New currencies and transfer platforms may provide a way for people, including those who rely on remittances, to escape the high transfer fees imposed by credit card and wire companies — and simply exchange money directly with one another around the world at almost no cost.

2. Bitcoin is complex and likely to remain so for a while.

There are people actively improving the security and transferability of Bitcoin, but its complexity still manages to keep it out of the reach of the technologically less sophisticated. The complexity of the system does not impede companies that wish to compensate their employees, at least in part, in bitcoins.

3. The bitcoin will be regulated- and that might be a good thing. In 2013, the Department of Homeland Security executed a seizure

warrant against the Japanese bitcoin Exchange, Mt. Gox, under the auspices of liquidity concerns.

According to Mickey Malka of "Ribbit Capital", which is investing in bitcoin ventures, regulation is not just inevitable — but desirable. He actually says it is likely to introduce a new level of credibility to the currency.

Either bitcoin will be our salvation from government manipulated, regulated, and taxed forms of money, or it will, at some point, fall from favor (whether engineered or from loss of belief in the coin).

In any case, if one is cautious in dabbling in this new commodity or currency, one may just be able to stay ahead of the crash of the dollar, without having to stockpile worthless paper or large stores of precious metals.

I think, at this point, I would prefer to trust in the age-old currency of gold and silver. They are currently at a historically low selling price for both gold and silver. When the dollar fails, the value of gold and silver (in dollars) will skyrocket as the demand for it increases.

**What Alternatives Do We Have Beside Bitcoins**
**When the Dollar Is Worthless?**
If you will remember, we earlier discussed the first form of trade, which did not include a currency. One person would either trade an item they had with something they desired from another person, although that may have been difficult, at times, because you may not have had an item desired by the person who has the commodity or service you offered.

Bartering, however, is a valid and valuable way to operate without government or bank-issued money. When the dollar is no longer viable and especially if we no longer have access to things like bitcoin, foreign currency, gold or silver, you will likely have something around the house or property of value. Perhaps you have some skill that will be valuable to someone who has produce, dairy, meat, etc.

Even if all you can do is rake a yard, sweep walkways, weed gardens, or use a wrench, there will be people who will need your skills and would be willing to provide you with food, clothing, oil, or whatever you might need in return.

It is difficult to imagine a world in which money is not what is used to do business or take care of your needs. It is even more difficult to imagine life without heat, water, electricity, all of which will be in doubt if we no longer have the availability of some kind of currency.

Undoubtedly, the people in power (sometimes it is difficult to define them just as the government) will come up with some way to exchange the worthless dollar for something perhaps we can have faith in and believe in.

It might be digital, it might be a different color and might be named something other than the dollar, but it's acceptance for the long term will be dubious.
Most likely, it will be something that provides stricter monitoring of the American people and more control over what they buy and how much they have.

Even if we have taken the precaution of putting our money into assets in other countries, there is still the question of whether we will be able to bring the benefits of such assets to this country.

There are already states that are providing alternatives to the disappearing dollar. Texas and Arizona, for instance, have passed laws allowing gold and silver to be used as legal tender in those states. That would, by far, be the most comprehensive means of dealing with a valueless dollar.

# Precious Metals and Other Assets Not Linked To the Financial Market.

**True Money**

We have talked a great deal about money in this book. Money, in most instances, has been shown to be an imaginary means of providing compensation for goods and services.

It is imaginary, because it is dependent on one believing in the credibility of the issuing entity, and the imputed value applied by that entity. As we have seen, by the examples past and present, of the people losing faith in the money market they deal in, the stability of this paper money is tenuous at best.

It is a form of secondary barter where one is given paper notes that imply value for services rendered or products sold, and which can then be bartered or traded for other services or products needed.

As long as everyone is in agreement that those notes are actual instruments of value, the system works fine. In a real transaction of value where there is a middleman (in our case that middleman is the
government) for the secondary trades, we would sell a good or service to the middleman, who would give us something of intrinsic value, like gold or silver, and that middleman would turn around and resell that good or service to a third party who would give the middleman a little more than what he had paid for that commodity.

All parties would come away with a benefit. In the case of the fiat currency used by different countries, the middleman (the party that provides the money, which has no real value) is facilitating the transaction from one person to the other, but there is technically no benefit to the middleman, except for the implied trust both of the other parties of the transaction seem to have in the middleman.

In this case, the middleman only benefits by being able to tax the parties involved. The money earned is taxed as income tax and the money received is taxed as sales tax. That is the benefit the government has in return for supplying the medium of exchange and taking on the risk of assuring the value is there to support the trust.

Throughout history, the main way to avoid this three party system and retain all the value, is by having gold and silver used as the medium of exchange. Since it facilitates a transaction that requires no middleman, there is no tax charged by an issuer of that medium.

Even when that gold or silver is in the form of a twenty dollar gold piece or a silver dollar, it is the intrinsic value of the metal, which is only certified as to purity and weight by the issuer, that the buyer and seller are interested in, and those are not always able to be traced or taxed by the middleman.

Today, both gold and silver are available in bullion coins of varying weights. One can get tenth ounce, quarter ounce, half ounce, and one ounce rounds. The smaller the size, the more of a premium one pays for the coin, but the more useful in transactions and purchases are that are coins in smaller percentages of the value of the metal than coins in one ounce sizes.

If the monetary system goes belly up, the actual purchasing power of the precious metals will be set by the market, meaning those from whom you are buying a service or good.

If one ounce of "real money" (gold) is worth $5,000 in a coin shop, it should be worth $5,000 in actual purchasing power if you are looking to purchase from a private party.

If you are looking to purchase from a retailer, the best thing to do would be to sell the amount of any precious metal to a coin shop to pay for the goods you need.

If hyperinflation has set in, it would not be wise to sell more than you need for the day, because tomorrow the price of the goods could be substantially different.

Wise financial consultants will tell you to keep a certain amount of cash on hand, in case something happens and you have no more income. This is wise to an extent.

Obviously, if you keep five thousand dollars on hand and the groceries you need to purchase go from $100 to $5,000 in one month (which can easily happen in hyperinflation), the value of your $5,000 has effectively gone down to $100 in purchasing power within that month.

Since gold and silver will go up in value as the dollar goes down, it would obviously make sense to keep "real money" cash (gold and silver) on hand, rather than fiat currency.

Finally, you need to be aware of the fact that the volatility in the value of precious metals that would result from hyperinflation could make it difficult to find a coin or precious metals dealer that would be willing to buy your metal.

Plan ahead. Have enough to help through the trials that are coming, but try to have smaller coins or silver to use them directly as a medium of exchange. One can still purchase bags of "junk silver", which consists of pre 1965 silver coins of dimes, quarters, and fifty cent pieces. They are already cut up in size to make it easier to use to purchase goods and services.

### If Governments Think Their Money Is So Great, Why Are They Buying So Much Gold?
If you go to the bank and ask the personnel in charge, if it would be wise to purchase gold or silver, their answer would be "NO." They argue if you buy gold, it will most certainly go down in value and you would lose much of your investment.

Further, they argue you should leave your money in the bank where it is safe and at least pays minimal interest. Do governments agree with that assessment?

The fervor with which various and large and small governments are purchasing gold would belie the idea that fiat currency is all we need or that your money is safer in a bank. China reached a record purchase of gold, in the first quarter of 2013, of 11.3 million ounces (353 ton) of gold.

Russia now owns over 35 million ounces of gold and purchased 296,000 ounces of gold in April of this year, alone. In 2014, Russia acquired 173 tons of gold (which is 36% of the total central bank demand for 2014).

Regarding India, Bloomberg predicts India is going to have purchased/imported between 10 million and 14 million ounces of gold in the second quarter of the 2013 year.

The real uncertainty is China. Though there are reports on the recorded purchases of gold by China, no one really knows how much they have nor how much they are purchasing.

Their government is picking up virtually every ounce of gold produced in China, but there are no accurate records about how much that might be.

You see, it doesn't matter that the dollar has been the world's reserve currency for so many years.

The central banks of other governments want to protect themselves against the obvious coming devaluation of the dollar as it loses its reserve status. This concern is not just limited to the countries mentioned above.

Most of the major countries around the world are purchasing record amounts of gold. There are only a few countries, one of which is Germany, that are divesting themselves of any gold at all.

In 2013, the United States government claimed to own 8,100 metric tons (a metric ton is 2,200 American pounds) of gold in places like Fort Knox. That is an amount that would, at that time, be worth about $340 billion dollars in value.

That would be enough to fund the budget in America for one month. That is not much of a gold reserve.
Nevertheless, the treasury is not interested in selling the gold, at any price seen recently, to help pay down the debt.

Regardless of anyone's personal opinion of the current or future assessment on the value of gold, most governments are treating it like…well….gold! Paper currencies, in the meantime, are all just fiat, worthless, currency. It is all a house of cards.

The only foundation for any country's wealth is actual gold holdings and Gross Domestic
Product. That is unlikely to change as the value of paper money, in any country, continues to decline.

The fact is that if China finally sees fit to declare what their gold holdings and acquisitions are, it is likely the value of gold (related to the devaluation of the dollar) will go to several thousand dollars an ounce.

That may sound like a lot, but against a dollar that is worth less and less each month and year, if it takes ten ounces of gold to buy a car, today, it is likely it will still take ten ounces of gold to buy a car when the value of the dollar goes to zero.

There may be some favorable movement, in regards to value of gold, especially because the perceived advantages of having something of intrinsic value will increase. Time will tell.

**Is There Gold in Fort Knox?**
That is the question of the century.
*This article was first published in* February 2013 by LewRockwell.com and Peter Schiff January 20 2014.

The financial world was shocked this month by a demand from Germany's Bundesbank (Federal Bank) to repatriate a large portion of its gold reserves held abroad. By 2020, Germany wants 50% of its total gold reserves back in Frankfurt – including 300 tons from the Federal Reserve.

The Bundesbank's announcement comes just three months after the Fed refused to submit to an audit of its holdings on Germany's behalf. One cannot help but wonder if the refusal triggered the demand.
The impact of Germany's repatriation on the dollar revolves around an unanswered question: why will it take seven years to complete the transfer?
See more at: **www.Bit.Do/eu-money**

Why would the Feds not allow the German government to even see the gold held on their behalf? If Germany has over 300 tons of gold that is being held by the U.S., one would think it would not be harmful to at least let them see it.

Even if the gold had been hypothecated it would do no harm to see it. For that reason, many people question whether the Feds have actually sold the gold with the presumed certainty that they would be able to buy it back before the owner(s) decided to repatriate it.

In real estate, and other professions where the licensed party holds funds for a client, that would be called "co-mingling", which is illegal and punishable by loss of license, a dollar fine, and certain jail time.

Since, at this point, the Feds are not allowing anyone to audit the gold holdings in Fort Knox and New York, and since there is no one with enough legal clout to force the issue, I think it is safe to assume there is either no gold left in storage or enough is missing to make it obvious.

That is why the question, "Is there still gold in Fort Knox?" is the question of the century. Unfortunately it is one that may not get

answered soon. The immediate return demand of all the gold owned by
Germany and stored by the US would create a potential run on the Fed, with other countries seeing the writing on the wall and demanding their gold, too.

If the Fed still had the gold, that would create nothing more than a logistical problem, but solvable. You can decide for yourself if there is anything to the suspicion that the gold is gone.

**Can We Return To the Gold Standard?**
Although there is a movement by some to try to restore some kind of actual value to money by, once again, tying it to gold, it would be an action fraught with many problems.

In 1971, America came off the gold standard. Since then there has been higher unemployment, and a lower growth rate. No one knows, of course, whether all that would still have happened if we had not gone off the gold standard.

Another problem with going back on the gold standard is the amount of gold that would have to be collected to provide even a small percentage of gold for every dollar, printed or otherwise.

We are currently over 18 trillion dollars in debt. Although those dollars are fiat dollars, they would nevertheless be dollars that would have to be backed by gold.

Actual obligated dollar commitments, however, are closer to 100 trillion dollars. Backing that kind of debt with gold would require a great deal more gold that what would be available, even if we had access to much more gold.
All the citizens in America would not likely have enough gold to help, even if it were all confiscated.
Finally, and probably the most onerous, is if we were to back each dollar with gold, the immediate siphoning of gold from America would be staggering.

Every country that holds dollars for any reason would immediately want to exchange their dollars for gold. There would, unfortunately, be no benefit we would receive in return, except the reduction of our debt.

Certainly the politicians would not agree to that kind of arrangement. Any confiscation of gold or silver on the part of our government, right now, would be strictly that, a confiscation and a theft of our wealth, where it applies to gold or silver.

The poor would not likely care and the wealthy would most likely have made plans to harbor their wealth off-shore. It is the middle class, blue collar, populace that would suffer the most. Much of that class has small stores of gold and silver.

It is usually not enough to warrant the expense of setting up storage in another country, but enough to attract attention if one wants to sell or utilize it as a medium of exchange if things get tough and the dollar dries up.

# When Will the Dollar Loses Its Value And What Good Will
# Income Producing Assets Be?

**How Long Before the Dollar Goes To Zero?**
This is a great question. If one could accurately predict how long it will be before everyone recognizes there is no more value to the dollar than the paper on which it is printed, one could be fully prepared and perhaps even leave the country with his or her assets.

If one listens to the financial consultants mentioned at the beginning of this book, it will not be long. Some are predicting there will be a sudden recognition by the world at large and collapse within the next year. It might be driven by almost any international incident.

For example, if China declares what its gold holdings and acquisitions truly are, that could trigger a total rejection of the dollar in the international community.
When the Asian Infrastructure Investment Bank (AIIB) has contracted with enough countries to have all debts and transactions settled in the yuan, the current faith placed in the dollar will disappear.

At that point, America will have to purchase the yuan in order to make payment on oil, produce, commodities, and goods that are manufactured outside the US.

Since there are already over 57 countries having signed on as founding members at the time of this writing, it is a foregone conclusion that it will overtake the World Bank. Unlike the World Bank, there will be no veto power inside the AIIB.

America holds a limited veto power within the World Bank, making it the only country to have the power to run roughshod over other countries and transactions.

Although the dollar currently is just off a spike in value against other currencies, it is believed that its value will continue to decline. In fact, just as it is in Europe with the euro, the US is doing whatever it can to encourage that decline. It is argued that the less value the dollar has (or the euro in Europe) the better products will sell, since that makes our products cheaper by virtue of stronger foreign currencies.

**Will There Be Any Warning?**
This is perhaps one of the most vexing questions. You see, there have been ongoing warnings for the past fifty or more years. I believe the first profound warning was in the formation of the Federal Reserve
Bank.

That formation gave a private bank the right and responsibility to print money and control economic policies. Under Article 1, Section 8 of the Constitution, only Congress shall have the authority or power to, "To coin Money, regulate the Value thereof, and of foreign Coin, and fix the Standard of Weights and Measures;" and, "To provide for the Punishment of counterfeiting the Securities and current Coin of the United States;"
Under this constitutional requirement, granting the power to create money to the Federal Reserve was the first step in devaluing the dollar.

The chapter on the Creature from Jekyll Island explains more about how this constitutional requirement was corrupted and taken over by rich bankers in secret.

That was also the beginning of the end of the "Silver Certificates" and any other form of United States Currency that had any valid standard of backing from the government.

It has been reported, (although I have not been able to find any actual documentation on this) that President John F. Kennedy commissioned the printing of the United States dollar currency, which would have been outside the control of the Federal Reserve Bank.

It is sometimes theorized that it was for that reason he was assassinated. The threat to the Federal Reserve Bank and its control over our money was too great to ignore. It would have robbed them of the ability to print and dispense money, which upon repayment became their own money.

The counter-balance was to have been for them to re-convey the money that was repaid to them, back to the Treasury. Unless or until there is a full audit of the Fed, no one truly knows how much they have or where it all goes.

They operate outside the normal law for such things. They have apparently, on occasion, lent money to other countries, sometimes in the trillions, without any accounting for it.

When asked by Congress where the money went, their response is a simple, "We don't know." If ever an organization needed to be audited, it is the Federal Reserve Bank.

Further warnings that point to a crash of the dollar are more evident at the ground level. The government's spending of trillions of dollars it doesn't have, has resulted in our current 18 trillion dollar debt and nearly 75 trillion dollar unfunded liabilities. A trillion dollars is a number no one can truly comprehend. It is an artificial value that merely represents numbers, without there being any accountability.

Politicians have no real concept of that amount of money, but can easily comprehend the number "18." I don't know how much a trillion is, but I know we owe *18 of them.*

Since that amount of money is so many times more than the annual national budget, the ability of America to repay that debt to the nations they have borrowed it from is virtually nil. That means the dollar already has no value.

For it to have value, there would have to be something of value backing it. For a long time it was the full faith and credit of the United States. We no longer have any faith or credit when it comes to the federal budget.

Look at your grocery cart, when you go to the grocery store. How full is it when you purchase $100 worth of groceries now?

Compare that with how full it was only ten years ago for the same amount of money. It seems the amount you get for your money goes down every day. Is that not a sign the dollar is worth less, every time you shop?

So the answer to the question, "Will there be any warning?" is, we have had warning after warning. It is absolutely astounding that the American public has not yet panicked.

At the rate of increase in the debt ceiling, the frequency with which dollars are printed without increasing the backing for those new dollars, and the resulting loss of purchasing power for those dollars, the abstract value of the dollar is destined to reach a devastating "zero" before we know it.

It is for that reason I have decided to write this book. My fellow middle class, blue collar workers have been lied to, cheated, and have been subjected to onerous new taxing laws for so long, we just avert our eyes and continue on as though nothing were amiss.

There are things you can do to protect yourself and I have covered a lot of those things in this book. I have also attempted to educate you as to the whys and the need to counter the offense from our legislators. Again, I lament that you need to go further than I have in this book. Find out what financial consultants in the know are recommending to protect yourself and your financial status.

The steps Warren Buffet takes to protect many of his assets and his wealth are the same, on a smaller scale, as what you have to do to protect yourself.

Do not delay educating yourself in what is available for your protection.

The collapse could still be several years off, God knows they have been able to postpone it to the point of owing numerous trillions of dollars, or it could be this year.

## What Will Happen To Income Producing Assets?

Since income producing assets are one of the most obvious hedges against inflation, I think it would be important to understand what happens to those assets in the event of hyperinflation and the crash of the dollar.

In a report by USAGold, that discusses the causes and solutions of inflation and hyperinflation, the forward by Michael J. Kosares says,

*"The survivors of the German Debacle did so, as shown in the preceding chart, by purchasing gold early in the process. As a citizen and an investor, the best you can do is be prepared and hope that it doesn't happen here. This report of Germany's hyperinflation, originally published in 1970 by Scientific Market Analysis, could play an important part in your preparation process. There is little doubt it will affect your thinking."*

**(http://www.usagold.com/germannightmare.html)**

The referenced report is ended with a Final Note:

"By the end of the 1970's, double-digit inflation had ravaged the American financial landscape.
This forecast by Scientific Market Analysis was not only accurate, it was prescient, and the conclusions drawn enduring.

Only the very strict monetary policies of the Federal Reserve Bank during the 1980's under chairman Paul Volcker kept the nation from sliding into the hyperinflationary abyss, and those years became a period of relative calm.

The profligate fiscal policies of the United States government, however, continued unabated, and after the credit crisis of 2008, the Federal Reserve began openly and unapologetically monetizing the national debt through its quantitative easing program.

Since 2008, the overall national debt has grown to enormous proportions and so has the Fed's balance sheet of monetized assets. 'On a rolling six-month average, in fact,' says Royal Bank of Scotland's Drew Brick, 'the Fed is now responsible for monetizing a record 70% of all net supply measured in 10-year equivalents.

*This* represents a reliance on the Fed that is greater than ever before in *history*!' Hauntingly, as was the case during the early stages of the Nightmare German Inflation, 'events seemed to demand the printing of larger and larger issues of currency.' Such reliance, as Scientific Market Analysis argues above, cannot end well. MK"

In the report it reveals the people who held income property benefited, somewhat, from the inflation rate wiping out their mortgages. They did not benefit from the rents, since they were frozen early on. Their primary benefit, in holding on to the property, was in the possession of the property as an asset in the new economy.

Rents were then tied to the new currency and those properties became a source of value and income again.
Those who lost were the ones who had to sell at a greatly reduced rate to provide badly needed cash. Those people generally never recovered from the realized losses.

Further, many of the owners of income property ended up having to refinance their properties, after the inflation problem had been resolved, to provide sorely needed cash to recover from other encumbrances created by the period of hyperinflation.

Further, governments have an annoying habit of raising property taxes on properties to generate needed funds. This can, when taken to the obvious extremes, bankrupt property owners.

Clearly, properly positioning yourself with a low interest rate mortgages, which often are wiped out in hyperinflation, provides you the opportunities to have property virtually unencumbered by mortgage.
For that to work for you, it is imperative you have means other than the income properties to survive the financial storm.
We have already reviewed many of those methods and strategies. Just remember, this book is trying to prepare you for the worst. It is not meant to be a guarantee of success. Governments can, if they choose, wipe out even the best prepared.

During the Great Depression, there were many people who had to sell their properties. Many of the buyers were people who had a store of gold they were able to use as a medium of exchange at an extremely beneficial exchange rate.

Income properties were purchased for as little as fifty ounces of gold, to several hundred ounces of gold. At a fixed value of $32 per ounce, these properties were, relatively speaking, sold for very low prices. Many millionaires were made during that time.

If you have gold or silver available during a hyperinflation period when people become desperate to sell and get some cash, you could potentially pick up some very nice, albeit non-income producing at that time, properties that would benefit you greatly once the country's insolvency issues have been remedied.

# Conclusion

In this book, I have attempted to give you a background on how the monetary system came about, what events have led to today's insolvency, and why it is likely to end up in either hyperinflation or some kind of digital currency that subjugates the citizens to total scrutiny, or both.

For the country to switch to a digital currency does not, in any way, insure the American people will have any greater faith in that nebulous currency, nor is there anything that says other countries will recognize it or accept it in payment of goods.

If there is one thing I hope I have conveyed to you, it is this: make sure you plan for the inevitable. While we don't know exactly, in this technological day and age, when the other shoe will drop and how we will be affected by the continued federal, state, and bank mismanagement of our money and taxes, we do know that *something devastating is coming*.

Just as Germany had to pay more and more German marks for dollars, which they then had to use to pay off the reparations, we will, at some point have to pay more and more dollars to purchase the then reserve currency (probably the yuan) to pay off our debt to other countries and buy international goods.

If you are counting on the United States government to take care of these things for you, you will be greatly disappointed.

Even if we went back to the policies that worked for two hundred years, the amount of debt that has to be satisfied is unfathomable and impossible to meet. Politicians, even if they overcome their unjustifiable propensity to spend money we don't have, would have to find some way, besides taxing its citizens, to come up with almost unlimited funds to pay back the eighteen trillion and climbing debt.

It has been said that politicians have spent the money of our grandchildren and great grandchildren. The truth is, as the debt continues to increase from unrestricted spending, the potential of ever being able to reduce or eliminate the debt is less and less likely.

We, the American people, not only have the power but the obligation to stop the rampant spending. As the docile sheep we have shown ourselves to be, however, we will continue to rely on the government to make everything "go away".

The politicians must, after all, know what they are doing. Don't they have a crystal ball that tells them what to do and teaches them economics? What they have exhibited so far shows just how untrue that is.

Plan for the worst and you will not be disappointed if the worst doesn't happen. Lay up for tomorrow, not in diminishing dollars, but in things that are of value on their own.

While it is still possible, open accounts in other nations and, better still, in a currency that is not declining in value as are the dollar, euro, Swiss franc, and GB pound. Purchase gold and silver, even if it is only a coin at a time.

*Every time you get an extra $20, go out and purchase a silver dollar or an ounce of pure silver.*
Save and purchase gold coins, either in one ounce rounds, $20 gold pieces, or fractional ounces.

If you can amass ten gold pieces (of one ounce each) at the current $1200 per ounce (for a total of about $12,000), when it goes up to $5,000 per ounce, which is not all that unlikely, that would give you $50,000 in gold!

This could happen in a month or in three years. Whenever it happens, you will be glad you stored up something that has intrinsic value, instead of paper money, in the form of numbers at a bank, under the control of federal and state authorities.

It will be too late to argue with the government about who it belongs to. In fact, even a successful argument would only end up having you in possession of an ever declining dollar that is earning no interest.

The Bible teaches we are to be good stewards of that, which we have been given. It is in that vein I pray your success in taking the information in this book to heart.

I also pray you will use this book as a springboard to get you interested in more in-depth books on the same subject. This book only contains a fraction of the information and advice available.

You don't have to be rich to want to preserve what you have. You don't have to limit yourself to what the main-stream media presents as the United States economic condition.

In the last decade one can actually say you should have been 180 degrees off from what the media said or suggested. If we were in the 1960s, I would have said, "Invest, invest, invest. Do so in compounding interest accounts.

Allow your wealth to grow and reap the benefits of a healthy economy." That is no longer the case. There is no scenario I know of where America will not succumb to its own greedy, selfish, arrogant, self-inflicted cancer of economic idiocy. You do not have unlimited time to try to do things the way they did in the sixties.

If we are fortunate, we may have a year or ten years, during which time the all invasive inflation will continue to harvest our hard-earned, albeit minimal, wealth.

That is not much time to utilize the ever diminishing dollar to try to create an inflation-resistant nest egg.

My wife and I started preparing for this after the mortgage and real estate bubble collapsed stealing from us hundreds of thousands of dollars we had so carefully invested in time tried and proven real estate strategies.

Our retirement was virtually secured and our income was very comfortable. All that disappeared in a relative *twinkle of the eye*.

Although, by following the recommendations of some financial consultants, many of the ones mentioned early in this book, we not only managed to land on our feet (out of any real debt), but we are fully confident and intent on doing whatever is necessary to hedge for the coming implosion.

# For More Titles On This Topic Visit Us At:

www.2ndEmpireMedia.com

www.ingramcontent.com/pod-product-compliance
Lightning Source LLC
Chambersburg PA
CBHW070156290526
45789CB00002B/787